The Persimmon River Novel Series

Independence

Independence is a work of fiction. Names, characters, places, and incidents are the products of the author's imagination or are used fictitiously. Any resemblance to actual events, locales, or persons, living or dead, is entirely coincidental.

Revised portions of the following appear in the novel: "Gravity," *Poetry & Short Story Journal* Volume Seven (The Cuddy Family Foundation for Veterans, February, 2024); "Blue smoke war /White bones men," Op-Ed by Michael Lund, *Richmond Times-Dispatch*, May 30, 2021); "Bees" *Intima: A Journal of Narrative Medicine* (November 2020); "Walking the Chickens," *War Writers'* Campaign (2014); rpt. in the *Voices of War Anthology* (2015). "Tumbling Pigeons," in *How to Not Tell a War Story* (print edition, Beach-House Books; digital edition, Milspeak Books, 2012). *Growing Up on Route 66* (BeachHouse Books, 2000). I am grateful to friends in Tidewater Virginia and North Carolina who have educated me, a native Midwesterner, in the histories and cultures of this region. I have been fortunate that Marge Swayne has been willing to edit/proofread the final manuscript. Her knowledge of the subject and professional experience as a writer were invaluable. I especially thank the following individuals for responses and suggestions that have improved my writing: Carleton Davenport, William Frank, Elizabeth Hall Mc-Gill, Geoff Orth, Laura Pietkiewicz, Valerie Ormand, and always Anne Lund. Design assistance provided by John Lund.

Independence

Dancing with Time

by Taylor Curtis
(Michael Lund)

Glorybound Publishing
Camp Verde, Arizona USA
in the year 2024

Dedication

For American soldiers and their families, especially Eldon and Roy from the Greatest Generation; Stephen, Tim, Thomas, and Bernie from my own.

Book Reviews

About Michael Lund's work:

"Route 66, with its endless stream of traffic and modest roadside motels and restaurants, provides the backdrop [to his stories]. . . . His characters move from their small stretch of Route 66 into the world beyond."-- Nancy Beardsley, Voice of America

" . . . *[Route 66 Déjà Vu]* examines local, national, and international mid-twentieth-century problems that still exist to- day. Naturally, Lund writes about the Vietnam War. He served in-country as an Army correspondent in 1970-71. . . . . The book broadens . . . wartime perspective with stories told by friends who were soldiers and nurses. Similarly, the dialogue often sounds as if each pronouncement is a lesson about our nation's present or past behavior. . . . "—Vietnam Veterans of America *Veteran Books in Review II* December 2023

--"I highly recommend the stories in this book [*Eating with Veterans*] to all those drawn to serious writing about the Vietnam War and to seekers after the whole story—not just a narrow story told over and over again."— Vietnam Veterans of America's "Books in Review"

-- "He has a rare gift as a storyteller. Many of the stories [in How Not to Tell a War Story] are written in a point-counterpoint method, alternating passages set in Vietnam with passages set back home after the war. This technique shows how inextricably linked the past is to the present and how a soldier's war experiences permeate an ex-soldier's later life. . . . Thanks to Michael Lund for bravely going with his short stories where no other Vietnam War author has gone before."—David Willson

". . . was struck by how perfectly [*Growing Up on Route 66*] seemed to encircle (of course) the world of childhood and its heady veering toward adulthood. It's a loving and funny book . . . and made me recall with mingled pleasure and embarrassment."--Carrie Brown, author of *Lamb In Love* and *The Hatbox Baby*

--"As an adult, the narrator has a philosophical outlook. 'The road I've traveled has clearer landmarks when I look behind me than when I was moving forward.'" Tricia Mosser, *Missouri Life*

" . . . a howl with just enough of the serious to add contrast and spice."--William Hoffman, award-winning author of *Godfires*, and *Tidewater Blood*

--"Lund presents an entertaining story of small-town life-paperboys, the gentle aspects of life in a simpler time and the wonder of the people who make small towns the linchpin of America. Through the eyes of Mark Landon we find that the answers to the myriad questions of life and love aren't always easy to find."--Bob Moore, ROUTE 66 MAGAZINE

--"An extremely heartwarming and nostalgic look at young people's angst during this age of wonder." ROUTE 66 FEDERATION NEWS

--"A wonderfully well-wrought novel, set in a place that's still the stuff of myth, about coming of age in a simpler time when sex was giddily mysterious and life was filled with end- less possibilities." Bernard Edelman, editor of *Dear America: Letters Home from Vietnam* and *Centenarians: The Story of the 20th by the Americans Who Lived It*

Characters

Cathy (hospital administrator, nurse) and **Mark Nelson** (public relations officer): recently retired to a house on Water Street.

Louis (bank executive) and **Mary** (doctor): the Nelson children

He Who Travels Well: local character, descendant of Eastern NC Native Americans

"John Smith": retired spook/Navy Seal and Korean War vet

Raymond Winston: troubled but likable Vietnam veteran

Jimmy Winston: local police officer

Beverly Foster: attorney and handy-woman.

Charlene Brown: new to the community, retired Marine.

Patrick and **Vickie Martin**; **Carl** and **Klara Paterson**; **Anne-Harriet Reed**: "senior"seniors on Water Street, The men are WWII vets. All represent the Greatest Generation.

Sharlene: owner of Darlene's, beauty shop founded by her mother

Thomas Beard: local fireworks expert.

Douglas: cider donut maker whose Whole Donut Van travels through town twice a year.

Vernon Benson: long-time proprietor of Vernon's Hardware Store

Randy and Caro-*lyne* Lee: couple from the Northeast who buy small store as second home.

Linda: keeper of tumbling pigeons

Father Time: shop owner, specializing in beach equipment and specialty items

Miranda Simpson: granddaughter of Staffordshire couple, regular Staffordshire visitor

Dusty Sherman: handsome crop-duster pilot

Mark Barber: Mark Nelson's fellow Army correspondent in Vietnam

James Baldwin: pastor of Staffordshire Baptist Church

Patricia: his wife

Jefferson Douglas: pastor at the AME Church.

Rebecca: his wife.

Janice: leader of the Bird Book Club

Les Moore :chiropractor and tennis instructor

Staffordshire

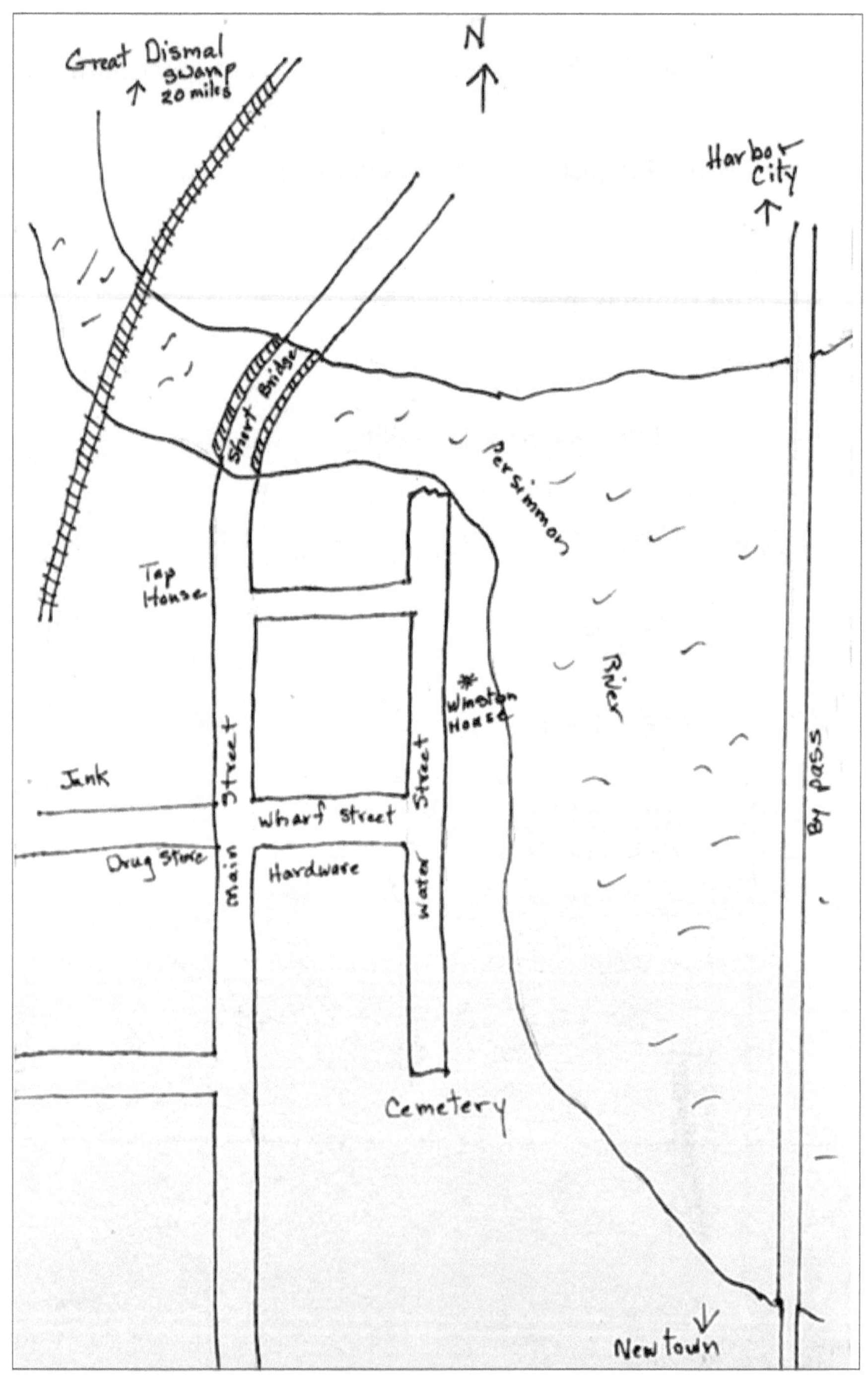

Prologue: "Alarm"

On the day they were finally ready to host the neighborhood's Independence Day party, Cathy and Mark were awakened by the smell of smoke. They threw on bathrobes and raced out into the hall. Sniffing the air, they walked past the three bedrooms where their two visiting children, spouses, and four grandchildren were sleeping. Nothing suspicious.

"I don't think it's upstairs," concluded Mark. "But I'd better check the attic." There were stairs at the end of the hall.

Cathy nodded. "It hasn't set off a fire alarm, so maybe it's not something inside. Meet me downstairs when you're done up here."

The back of the house faced the river, which was bordered in many places by cypress trees standing in the brackish water. In this flat tidewater terrain, both sounds and smells were carried by the wind from distant places across water and land. Smoke from swamp fires, burning fields after harvest, or tractors at work on the causeway repair project could invade the 115-year-old, poorly insulated, frame house—the Nelson's retirement home—at any time.

"You look outside," Cathy told Mark in a hushed but tense voice when he met her downstairs. "The kitchen appliances are fine. There's nothing wrong on the screen porch. I've even checked the fuse box and found nothing unusual/To herself she thought, "After all the headaches we've encountered trying to organize for July 4, we should have known something like this would happen at the last minute. And, given the way my husband has been acting the last few days, I'll be doubly lucky if our marriage doesn't go up in flames."

In the weeks leading up to the party they'd had to deal with confusion about the delivery of tables, chairs, and canopies. Competing, equally important holiday events had been announced. An emergency landing of a crop-dusting plane in an abandoned shopping center nearly ran them down. There had been the threat of wild animals entering town in search of food. Mark worried about PTSD episodes when veterans witnessed the innovative fireworks display. And Cathy had had to hold Mark as well as all the arrangements together.

His thoughts were equally dire, though part of him wanted to say, "I told you so," as he'd been ready to back out of the commitment at each of the complications they encountered. From the beginning, he had resisted the plan because, among other reasons, their wedding anniversary was July 5, and it seemed, to him at least, always to be neglected because of the national holiday.

In fact, he'd been reluctant to move to their house on the river full-time, and the July 4 hosting became one more reason for regret. Now they were hours away from fulfilling the promises they'd made to their senior neighbors to keep this half-a-century-old patriotic tradition alive in their tiny North Carolina village. Maybe he'd pull through, and life as usual—or at least as he preferred it—would return.

As he stepped through the back door, Mark turned on the floodlights illuminating the backyard, the garage, and the end of the driveway. One solar-powered, motion-detecting light showed him the deck he was standing on. No flickering flames were visible in the garage's window or beneath the wide double doors. Nothing out on the water indicated a vessel or an oil slick or drifting logs on fire. He couldn't hear the crinkling of any leaves or paper or plastic.. The cars in the driveway were dark and still.

Inside, Cathy again opened the stove, the microwave, and the door to the pantry and found nothing suspicious. She sniffed in the bathroom off the kitchen, walked down the hall past the guestroom, the dining room, and the living room, and encountered only pleasant reminders of their recent house-cleaning efforts and familiar old-house smells.

Drawn by the sound of a low chanting, Mark located the problem in their side-yard garden. The Native American swamp denizen, He Who Travels Well, was sitting cross-legged in the middle of the tomato plants, smoking his long-stemmed pipe, and serenading the plants.

"What are you doing out here?" demanded Mark. Then he said, "Wait. I need to tell Cathy the house isn't on fire."

In another few minutes, the Nelsons came out together. He Who Travels Well was in the same position, calmly puffing on his pipe, a cloud surrounding his head and the area where he was sitting. The bowl glowed, though the sun was beginning to light up the river to the east. Cathy and Mark smelled something odd in addition to the sharp tobacco smoke—something sour, rancid, like ammonia.

"Your plants are not well," He Who Travels Well offered.

Staffordshire did need rain, especially as the surrounding fields of soybeans, cotton, and corn were stunted as agriculture remained the dominant industry of this remote, rural county.

"My rain barrels ran out," Mark admitted. "But I doubt if smoke and . . . and, what is that other smell?"

"Dead flounder, of course. That's why I'm here, to keep away the raccoons, opossums, and other critters."

Cathy sighed. "Why did you have to do this now, so early

in the morning? We didn't know you were here. We could smell the smoke and we thought the house was on fire. Didn't you know we host the July 4 celebration today?"

Even as she said it, she realized the Weapemeoc people probably would have a different response to an event that meant the loss of independence for them, not its declaration. This man, perhaps the last of his tribe, was kind to them. They were, after all, relative newcomers. Other groups, justified in anger and aware of the increasing calls for reparation, could, for all she knew, be preparing to make some dramatic statement.

Of course, there were other elements of this old southern community that would be justified in seeking reparation after so many years of inequality. The Nelsons hadn't gotten to know enough people in other neighborhoods to judge the intensity of resentment.

"These plants do not recognize dates on a calendar," replied the browned man wearing his customary flat-brimmed, felt hat, faded camouflage plants, and shirt. "They note the angle of the sun, the temperature of the air, and clouds bearing water. They need to be free."

"Free?" growled Mark. "Plants? Next, the rocks will assert their right to liberty!"

One of his complaints about the community's planned celebration was that everyone—and every group—wanted special rights as part of the idea of independence. Freedom to worship, social mobility, gun rights, unrestricted trade, open borders—you name it.

Cathy took Mark's arm. "It's okay. We shouldn't have panicked. This is not a place where things get out of control. We'll go in and put on some coffee. When you're . . . um . . . done out here," she said to the garden protector, "come inside and join us."

"You are most kind," replied He Who Travels Well between puffs.

Mark would never tell Cathy—or anyone except perhaps a fellow vet—that the odd smell of He Who Travel Well's homegrown tobacco mixed with the rot of fish carcasses brought back unsettling memories from his tour in Vietnam. As an army correspondent, he was seldom close to the vegetation blasted by artillery, air strikes, and grenades, but it seemed his nose too often filled with acrid odors.

When Mark had spotted someone in his garden, his first thought was that it was Raymond Winston, who'd grown up in Staffordshire—in fact, in the very house the Nelsons now owned. Ray had shared a few tales about his time in Vietnam, one of which included a deliberately set fire. Of course, Mark could not tell how accurate his stories were. It was not that Raymond meant to deceive, but his memory wasn't always trustworthy after too many years of alcohol and drug use.

When Mark asked Ray if he had been the instigator of the mess hall fire, his friend seemed to forget what he'd been talking about. He slid into a story about his wartime love, Dolly, an entertainer with the American Red Cross. During one stand-down, she had singled him out to join her on stage.

Mark was relieved to see, though, that the smoke was innocent, the danger only in his mind. After all, as Cathy had said, this was not a place where things got out of control—was it?

Coming into the family room, He Who Travels Well announced, "Your plants are responding."

"You will get all the credit," smiled Cathy. To herself she added, please heal my husband also.

It would, in fact, be a good year for all their crops, though Mark felt cool nights, frequent showers, and a bit of Miracle-Grow were as responsible for the yield as their neighbor's ritual. There would be mix-ups, of course--who was supposed to give a welcome speech? And interruptions, like another surprise surfacing of a scuba diver in the river, did occur. Distractions came along. A college student, for instance, lured older men to empty upstairs bedrooms for amusement. But the Independence Day celebration would be a success.

Whether the neighborhood, the town, or the nation would follow through on the promise of a new union—that all "are created equal, that they are endowed by their Creator with certain unalienable Rights, that among these are Life, Liberty, and the Pursuit of Happiness"—would have to be be seen. And whether there would be any confirmation of the Nelson's marriage with a suitable anniversary celebration was very much in question.

Chapter One: Smith

Earlier that summer Mark and Cathy Nelson had been weighing the decision to host the neighborhood's 50-year-old July 4th celebration when a man wearing a wet suit and snorkeling gear, including oxygen tank, surfaced thirty feet from their bulkhead. Mark happened to be standing at the end of his dock, contemplating a canoe trip over to the cypress swamp a quarter mile south.

At first, Mark thought it was a turtle he was seeing, the dark round shape of the red-bellied species indigenous to the area rising to the surface. Then he wondered if the emerging figure might be a mullet, the jumping fish also common in the region. It was not likely to be a dolphin, though they could appear in this river when low rainfall brought white fish upstream, a tasty meal for the larger salt-water species.

The man (perhaps woman?) stood up in the water, less than four feet deep where he was, pulled up his mask, and announced, "Don't be alarmed, my friend. I'm one of the good guys."

His smile and friendly manner were reassuring. "Well, I am, too," Mark smiled back. Having been told to expect unannounced visitors coming by water to the neighborhood, he asked, "What brings you to our shores?"

The diver waded slowly toward the dock, water running down his face. He was not carrying a spear gun or explosive device in his hands, which he raised with palms facing forward. "Simple surveillance today. I make regular rounds to be sure they're not infiltrating our defenses."

"They?" Mark asked.

"The Russians, of course, the Communists." He paused about ten feet from the end of the dock, his expression showing surprise that he had to explain. Mark said, "Ah! I see. Good to be on the lookout." He shaded his eyes and scanned the horizon. "I would have expected them to come by surface or air, though."

"That's what they count on—lack of attention to alternatives. You know the Germans sent their submarines this way from the Atlantic during World War II. The Russians are following their example in many ways. Now, give me a hand there, will you. This gear is heavy out of the water." He'd reached the foot of the dock ladder and extended a hand up to Mark. "Smith's the name. Or at least you can call me that."

To Mark it sounded like he was saying, "Bond, James Bond." Mark concluded that this man was no danger—well, to anyone another than himself. So, he helped him up.

"If you don't mind, I'd like to sit in one of your chairs there and rest a bit." He gestured toward the small wooden picnic table with lawn chairs around it.

"Sure. And feel free to pull off your flippers if that will make it easier." His feet flapped awkwardly on the dock boards, catching on the gaps. They boosted travel in the water but held it up on land.

"They hate our country, you know," Smith asserted, sitting heavily on the lawn chair. "Always have. It's our freedom they can't stand, puppets of the state the way they are. They're always trying to identify our weak spots, get inside our perimeter of the Constitution."

"Can't say I disagree with that. Putin's made himself a leader for life and is clever in expanding his influence . . . although, Staffordshire, it seems to me, would be an odd choice for establishing a foothold in the country. We're a bit out of the way."

"Lemonade?" asked Cathy, walking down the bank toward them with a tray, a pitcher, and four glasses. "Mid-afternoon, I always like to sip a drink in the shade of these beautiful cypress." She gestured up. The sun was behind the top branches to the west.

"Why, that's mighty kind of you, ma'am. I think I may have gone a bit farther than I should today. A man of my age, you know."

Mark had been entertained by this almost comic character, but his wife's invitation to join them in refreshments irritated him. He was always cautious about engaging in new relationships, falling back on the familiar and comfortable.

The diver pulled off his cap, and Mark saw thin strands of white hair stuck to his scalp. His face had grey stubble and considerable wrinkles.

"Where," Cathy asked. "Where . . . um . . . where did you . . . put in?"

"Usual place, where my cabin is."

"And that's . . ."

"Friend, I don't tell everyone that—security, you know. And you're new here, no offense."

"No offense taken," smiled Cathy. "It's good to know someone has our safety in mind. And takes measures to preserve it." She turned and mouthed, "No negativity," to Mark. "You make your rounds regularly? We are, as you say, somewhat new, and no one has told us we have an underwater surveillance team . . . er . . . force. Are you with Sandy Point, the military base down at the end of the river?"

He eyed Mark carefully, "Can't comment on that. I do the river daily, but in sections, here about once week. And only a few know about what I do. I hadn't meant to 'come out,' as you will, today, but I may have gotten a bit disoriented. If the tank malfunctions, a diver might become a bit confused with low oxygen. I had intended . . . to come ashore down in the swamp." He gestured toward the place Mark had thought about taking his canoe.

So," Cathy mused, "you disappear a mile or more downriver and navigate . . . how?'

He smiled. "A good question. But there's an easy answer. There are landmarks on the river's bottom as there are up on land. You learn to map the bed as you would a stretch of wilderness." He winked at Mark. "They teach you that in Navy

Seal training, so you won't get confused."

Mark was beginning to wonder if this man wasn't confused about many things. "I'm sorry, but I don't think we've told you our names, and we should be polite: Mark and Cathy Nelson. And you're Smith?"

"You can call me Captain John Smith. Not my real name, of course, but I can't let you know that—for security reasons. Only three people in the world know who John Smith is— one's in prison, one's in South America—somewhere—, and one's in the White House."

Mark gave a little bow. "In that case, we consider ourselves honored."

Cathy said, "I was always told that swimmers are supposed to wait an hour after eating to go back in the water, but could I get you something to eat, a snack?"

"That's very kind, but I need to be back on duty. And, by the way, that 'hour after eating' does not apply to people like me."

He looked around to be sure he would leave nothing behind. Mark took the opportunity to ask, "There's something I've been wondering about in regard to your . . . mission. You look as if you could be retirement age, but here you are with what seems to me a 24/7 schedule. Don't you feel a bit restricted?"

He stood up, laughing. "Oh, Mr. Nelson, one is never restricted serving his country." He started toward the dock, his flippers trailing by their straps from one hand. Then he turned back. "I'll let you in on another secret. I see you have a canoe there, and I'll bet when you get out on the water, away from land and the daily demands of yard care, shopping, cooking, cleaning, you feel a deep sense of relaxation."

"Well, now that's true."

"Um-hm. And one of the factors that makes you feel this way is the freedom you have out on the water to go wherever you want. You do have to pay attention to wind and current, but there's not much traffic in this quiet river to hamper your way. Am I right?"

"You are right." Mark had felt that sense of openness strongly when he was out on Patrick's sailboat; but the canoe also allowed him to drift off in his thoughts as well as in his journey. When Cathy's ease in this new community seemed too much an indictment of his struggles with adapting, he retreated to the water. And it was true that this area had been spared the development—or exploitation—most places this close to the sea had suffered.

John Smith winked. "What you feel is just a tiny taste of what you get underwater, where no one even sees you, knows you're there. You glide this way, then that, just like the flounder, the bass, the perch. You're unmoored, so to speak, from guidelines, free of road signs, a being off the grid of ordinary space and time. Think of your dolphin jumping straight up from the water —full of joy at its freedom. It's a picture to remember."

"It would be romantic," said Cathy, "if you weren't responsible for protecting us."

"It's a calling, ma'am. It started when I volunteered to serve in Korea years ago. I stayed in nearly forty years, then transitioned to contract work with the Coast Guard and . . . and, well, agencies that have operations all over the world. I sing a song of freedom wherever I go."

With that, he turned around at the end of the dock and stooped to put his flippers back on. Standing straight, he adjusted his head covering and his mask, then blew air out the snorkeling tube. He raised two fingers to his forehead in fare-well, held his goggles in place, and toppled backwards into the river.

They watched for a few minutes, thinking they might see some bubbles or wake from his flippers, but they couldn't be sure. The waves slapped gently against the bulkhead.

Cathy said, "You know, I was thinking we'd go play some tennis today, but this is a little disorienting. Did it really happen?"

"I think it did. Though I'm not sure I can accept John Smith's backstory."

"No negativity, now—especially where our veterans are concerned."

She came from a military family. Four of her uncles had served in for WWII and the youngest enlisted but not in time to serve in combat. She was active in groups that provided support to military families.

"Right. But I say we keep this to ourselves, at least for now."

"To be sure," Cathy agreed. "For purposes of national security."

Chapter Two: Raymond

A few days later, Mark encountered another man he'd never seen before, this one sleeping on the floor of their garage. At least, he hoped he was just sleeping, not dead. Moving closer, he smelled alcohol, heard snoring, saw the chest rising and falling. So, he backed out cautiously, closed the door behind him, crossed the yard, and went into the kitchen.

"Just a note," he said to his wife Cathy, setting a paper bag on the counter between the kitchen and the breakfast nook. "There's a stranger sleeping in the garage this morning. I'm not sure this bodes well."

His words signaled resignation at another invasion of his comfort, just what he'd predicted before yielding to Cathy's insistence that now was the time to settle permanently in this little riverside town.

"Hmm," she responded. "John Smith?"

"I don't think so."

"Okay. Remember: no negativity."

Since they'd seen a sign with this maxim through the drive-in window of Bojangles out on the bypass, they'd used it jokingly to keep their spirits up as the adjustment to retirement had been harder than they'd expected, even for Cathy. The move from Virginia to North Carolina made Mark feel rootless, but he tried not to let his anxiety lead to open conflict with his spouse "of long standing." (He refused to use the term "old" for her or friends they'd had for years.)
Cathy said about the guest in their garage, "This is probably just someone who had a few too many last night at the tap house, got confused about where he was, and found a convenient place to rest. He'll wake up and be on his way."

The Nelsons lived on a quiet residential street, but the town was so small they were only a block and a half from the Main Street businesses—one of which was Persimmon River Tap House.

After picking up breakfast at the drive-through (Bojangles cinnamon biscuits were good!), Mark had found the unexpected tenant resting—comfortably, it seemed—in the 100-year-old building.

He told Cathy, "I saw the door partially open and went to check. The intruder was lying flat on his back, wearing worn camouflage pants and an old Army fatigue jacket."

"Hmm. Well, I say we eat first and discuss our options second," offered Cathy, opening the bag and placing a coffee thermos on the table in the breakfast nook. Although they were more than forty years married, he still marveled at her composure in dealing with the unexpected.

Mark agreed to put off confronting the situations (man in garage and decision on the July 4 event), but what ate away at his composure (while he ate away at his pastry) was a gnawing memory from his time in Vietnam: Bruce asleep (at least not dead, at least not yet) on the floor of the sound studio in Vietnam when the brass arrived.

He said to his wife, "A bit of an oxymoron, isn't it, now that I think about it: 'No Negativity'? Being against something—even negativity—is itself negative."

Cathy said, "It's also a double negative that some say results in a positive." Now she chuckled, "So, positivity as opposed to negativity, right?"

Mark acknowledged that in the new world of trite tweets, blaring web advertising, and debased social discourse this was effective communication: short, humorous, pointed. And he knew it was topical. Ever since 9/11 a national unease had emerged, characterized by a discourse of ridicule and insult. The country was so divided no one knew what the future held.

When they'd enjoyed a second cup of morning coffee, Mark asked Cathy, "So, just wake him up or ask the police to come by and quietly escort him to a better place?"

"Maybe it would be easier if I talked to him," she said standing. "You know, I'm not threatening, and you can be watching from . . . from here." She pointed to where she was by the window and then out to the garage, not twenty-five feet away.

"He could be more than drunk. You don't need to take the risk."

"Oh, you're just being the man."

He grimaced. "Well, yes, but your martial arts skills are limited." She had gone to take the woman's self-defense course at the Y, ending up learning to salsa.

"As if you're ready to take on intruders," she huffed.

"Listen, we know nothing about this guy, who may have escaped from that prison outside Harbor City. Why chance it?"

Before Cathy could object, Mark was out the door and crossing the yard to the garage. This time he deliberately made enough noise to rouse anybody who might be there. Swinging back one of the two large doors, he faced a man brandishing a pitchfork. Well, Mark's own pitchfork.

"Oh, easy there, friend," he said, raising both hands and backing up a step. "I'm just . . . um, checking the gas for the mower."

His guest scanned the garage. "We don't keep it here—danger of fire, you know."

We? thought Mark. He said, "Ah, you're right. It's in the . . ."

"Tobacco curing shed," he gestured over his shoulder. There was no tobacco curing shed on the property. Given the history of this rural county, though, perhaps there'd been one in the past.

While the stranger was acting as if this were his home, he didn't appear threatening. Grey hair, wrinkled face, bony hands, and a bit of a stoop suggested someone Mark's age or older.

And now he leaned the pitchfork against the wall beside the shovels and rakes. "You've got things pretty orderly here. You the new handyman?"

Mark decided to go along. "Well, yes. Probably only temporary, you know, now that you're back."

The man seemed puzzled. "I've been away? Yeah, I guess so. These days I get . . . um, confused some. So, anyway . . . breakfast?"

Mark saw the man's eyes focusing over his shoulder. Cathy was smiling and putting a cup of coffee on the patio picnic table. "I was just going to fix us some bacon, eggs, and toast," she called. "Come over. Sit, sit, have some coffee."

Mark's eyes went wide. The stranger did as he was asked and himself asked, "Sugar?"

"Sure. And how many eggs do you take?"

Both Mark and Cathy were keeping their distance from him (a pitchfork's length, perhaps). Mark was again trying to control his irritation at Cathy's welcome of a complete stranger into their yard, if not their house.

"Eggs? Why, six, ma'am." The unknown man was inspecting the side yard garden. "got a lot of work to do today." Mark winced, as he'd not put enough time into it to be able to anticipate much of a harvest.

While the Nelsons' 120-year-old house faced Water Street, it backed up on a wide, shallow Tidewater river. The garage in the side yard was originally reached by a U-shaped drive that went around the house. But a deck off the kitchen in the '90s had covered the bottom of the U.

Mark kept repairing the garage rather than replacing it, a desire to maintain the order of the past. When he came back from overseas, he was reassured that the country was still there, not blown to pieces as so much of Vietnam had been.

"Say," the stranger asked as he used a piece of toast to wipe up the last of his eggs, "who's hosting the Fourth of July fest this year? I know it's been here a number of times. But, sorry. You probably won't know about that, being just temporary, not really a resident."

Mark hesitated. "I think I heard . . . I don't think it's been decided yet. It kind of conflicts with our wedding anniversary, and I've been reviewing some options for an appropriate venue around here."

That wasn't true, but now that he thought about it, he might use the idea to leverage himself out of the role of host.

Mark went on. "Now, let me ask you something. I'm kind of new in these parts. What's the . . . um, history of this house?" He gestured at what he knew was named "The Winston House," as the historic society had provided a small sign that also indicated it had been built in 1905.

"Why, my grandfather had this place built before the First World War, and someone in the family has lived here ever since. We run the peanut oil mill, down Third Street."

"I see." The mill had burned years ago, and the site become a little-used town park. "But you've not been here all that time, am I right?"

"Went off to war, sonny, and came back not quite right. Vietnam, '66-'67. I kind of dropped out for a time, I guess, after that. Sorry to mention it, ma'am, but I turned to drink some. And gambled. After a while my days became my nights, know what I mean?"

"I think I do," agreed Mark. He'd been in Vietnam, too, and sympathized with those experiencing disorientation returning home. "But you're . . . better now?"

"I'm used to being a bit . . . under the weather . . . most of the time. Hey, Jimmy." He was greeting a policeman who'd come around the house without Mark noticing. Cathy must have called the station, which was, like everything else, less than a ten-minute walk away.

Mark concluded that, with the authorities stepping in, the morning, which had started out negative, might turn positive after all.

He couldn't know that this was only the first in a series of surprises that would disturb his life all the way to and beyond the Fourth of July. The sense of forces undermining the social order—as well as his marriage—would grow to the point that he would become physically ill just days before July 4.

Chapter Three: Beverly

"Hi, Raymond," said Officer James Winston. Mark read the name on his uniform. He'd learned that a few of the old families had many members living in and around the town. His own children had settled in eastern Virginia, about two hours from where they'd grown up.

The policeman smiled at the visitor. "Good to see you. Back in town for a bit?"

"Well, yeah, I guess so," agreed Raymond. "Maybe stay at the house for a while," nodding toward the kitchen, "until I get my bearings." He rubbed the grey stubble on his chin. "Can't quite remember where I'm coming from."

"Tell you what, Ray, why don't you walk with me over to the station. I think William is there. Why, he'll want to talk to you!"

"William is? Damn, I've not seen him in years." He rose to go. "Folks, I appreciate the use of the bed and a meal. You all are nice people. And I guess I'll see you a bit later."

Officer Winston cupped Raymond's elbow and steered him toward the street.

Mark opened his eyes wide to Cathy. "Well, now, that's interesting."

"It looks as if he won't be a problem for us, at least. You see? You were worried about nothing, as usual."

He picked up the plate and cup Raymond had been using and started toward the kitchen. "However, there's . . . as we say . . . 'more to the story.'"

"Something from your past or the town's?"

"Mine. Have I ever told you about Bruce, my fellow Army correspondent in Vietnam?"

"No, but you really haven't told me much at all about your tour."

They had married five years after he returned. Before then he had used the GI Bill to get an MBA and went to work as a public relations officer for a small-town bank in Virginia (which was taken over by Wachovia, which was taken over by Wells Fargo, which closed everything but its ATM before he retired).

"I don't think so. I hope it's not a sad story."

"Let's leave it for a later time. But I will confess, Raymond reminds me of Bruce."

He and Mark had traveled the country, their assignment to get "uplifting" stories for the people back home. At Long Binh they lamented the disasters that weren't reported and marked days off their short-timer calendars. Mark's philosophy had been to do the job with the lowest possible profile. Bruce gambled that he could avoid injury (or worse) in the field and official scrutiny of his actions in the rear—both of which included pretty heavy drug use.

He and Cathy learned more about garage guest Raymond the next afternoon when Officer Winston came back to the Nelsons'. "Sorry Raymond bothered you, folks. But he's harmless. Goes off on binges, forgets where he is, can wake up most anywhere in the county."

"A town character?" suggested Cathy.

"That's right, ma'am, one of . . . several. He's a relative of mine, second cousin twice removed or something like that. He's getting on in age, though, so he disappears more and more often. Which is kind of funny, as he sometimes thinks he's a magician—making things vanish and come back. My wife is a nurse and says he's failing faster now. Not been kind to his body all these years."

"He didn't really bother us," Cathy said reassuringly. "He was, actually, quite polite." Looking aside, she mouthed the phrase "No negativity" to Mark.

"That's good, that's good. He generally shows up on the farm, just west of town, less than a mile. This was . . . unusual. So, thanks for being understanding."

When he'd gone and Mark and Cathy returned to the family room, she asked, "So, what are you thinking about being . . . 'understanding' with hosting the Independence Day event?"

He gazed out the picture window toward the river. There were four ancient cypress trees forty feet off their deck and another forty feet farther, next to river. The concrete bulkhead there had been put in by the WPA in the 1930s. Mark knew it should be replaced, but a goofy nostalgia kept him postponing the project.

"To be honest, I'm a bit anxious, not sure what to expect . . . what?"

Cathy had held a hand up and cocked her head toward the front of the house. "I think I heard someone knock. Will you check?" The family room/kitchen was at the back of the house, and a spacious hall went past dining room and living room to the front porch. Hard of hearing himself, and the doorbell out of commission, Mark might well have not heard a sound.

He opened the door to a slender woman perhaps in her mid-fifties wearing neat work clothes with a full tool belt around her waist. "Hi," she said. "I'm Beverly Foster, and I understand you're looking for a handyman . . . well, perhaps a handy woman."

Not wanting to appear inhospitable, Mark ushered her into the hall. "I hadn't advertised, but it's possible, now that I think about it, that we might need someone on a temporary basis."

"Raymond, at the police station, said whoever had been here was moving on."

"Ah, Raymond." He smiled. "Cathy," he called. "Come here a minute, please." Then he turned back to the potential handy woman. "I'm Mark Nelson, and this is Cathy."

The two women smiled and exchanged greetings. Mark explained to Cathy, "Ray told Beverly that our 'former helper' is . . . um . . . moving on and that we might need a handy . . . woman."

Cathy nodded. "It has occurred to me that if—if—," she bowed to Mark, "if we are going to take on the July 4 celebration, maybe we could use some extra hands."

"I know the property pretty well, Mr. Nelson. As a teenager, before college and law school, I used to take care of lawns along Water Street. And I realize you will have to make adjustments to host . . . what do you think, 75 to 100 guests?"

Mark glanced at Cathy and could see that she, like him, had been thinking more in the 40 to 50 range. She reached a hand out to Beverly and said, "Let's go back to the kitchen and talk."

Seeing Cathy's look, Mark realized Beverly was already hired. Whether they were to host the event or not, his own role as handyman would be reduced, and he resented the lessening of his traditional masculine role.

He did wonder why a lawyer was doing manual labor, though he understood that the town's diminishing population could support only a limited number of professionals. He had obscured that fact when he encouraged their daughter, a pediatrician, and his son, a bank executive, to move down here. But their children--Mark and Cathy's four grandchildren--were in schools they liked, and they all had their places in social networks.

Each family had made several long weekend visits during the past year, the kids enjoying swimming and canoeing. But it was easier for Cathy and Mark to drive up to Chesapeake every month or so and see both families at the same time.

He stepped onto the porch to look one more time at the doorbell. It was not the one originally installed years ago, but a remote device that transmitted a wireless signal from the button on the door to an interior ringer. He assumed he might as well replace it with a new one.

As he entered the family room, he heard Beverly explaining, "I'll work my own hours but give you a full twenty each week. I have some other responsibilities here right now, so I'll need flexibility. I don't cook, serve food or drinks, but I can help clean up and cart away trash."

Cathy smiled. "That will suit us just fine. Mark, she grew up down the river, back before it was developed. So, she has ties to the community."

The Persimmon River flows twenty miles southeast from the Great Dismal Swamp. After years of commercial exploitation, some of the wilderness area upriver had been restored and now harbored black bears, bob cats, otters, weasels, reptiles, amphibians, and hundreds of bird species. Mark liked living close to such a wilderness, as if every day an exotic creature might swim up to their bulkhead or another come ambling down Water Street—not John Smith, however.

"That's good. Maybe you can fill us in sometime on the history of the region between the Persimmon and the Little River."

Northeastern North Carolina is shaped geographically by peninsulas created by parallel rivers flowing southeast into the Albemarle Sound. No one drives down those stretches of land other than locals, so these peninsular communities retain much of their out-of-the way, pre-World War II character.

Beverly laughed, "You may learn more than you want—I grew up with some characters; a few still hide out in the area. But I won't tell you where their stills are . . . er, were."

"To be honest, we might find moonshiners more interesting that the retirees from the Northeast building new homes out at the Colony." This was an upscale development where the Persimmon River spilled into the Albemarle Sound. With a country club, golf course, marina and restaurant, residents generally kept to themselves.

After Beverly left, Mark asked Cathy, "So, you've," he stressed the second person, "made a decision that with Beverly's help we can pull off the project?"

"Why not?" she said. And then what would become famous last words, "How much trouble can it be?" And Mark shivered.

Chapter Four: Charlene

The next day Cathy proposed they play their regular game of Scrabble out on the screen porch. The house was built before air conditioning, so the Z-shaped porch was designed to catch the river breeze. A former owner had enclosed potions of the porch beside the kitchen (expanding that space to make it a family room) and the master bedroom upstairs (creating a study). There was still an L-shaped screen porch in back and a larger Z-shaped front porch.

"Maybe as we play," suggested Mark, "we can review what you and Beverly discussed in terms of hosting the neighborhood party."

The Independence Day tradition had started sometime in the 1950s. Many of the men on Water and Main Streets had served overseas in WWII and wanted to restore the sense of community they'd experienced growing up during the Depression.

"Community" was characterized by racial divisions typical of small Southern town. There was no open hostility, but everyone seemed to accept that your "neighborhood" identified your race. The Nelsons had met no neighbors of color on Water Street.

Cathy said, "It would be a good way to learn about our immediate neighbors."

They'd realized that many veterans chose to retire to this area. A lot had served in Norfolk area Navy bases; and there was a smaller contingent of Army vets who'd found cost of living and lifestyle amenable.

The Best Generation worked hard as town officials, bankers, tradespeople, teachers, and lawyers, many of them living in the houses where they'd grown up. The population had less than 2,000 in 1900, and it was roughly the same a century later. The idea of revitalization was always met by a fear of change, but the need was becoming more apparent. The women mostly returned to their pre-war roles as wives and mothers.

"What I recall," said Mark, "is someone—people at the end of the street?—haul in a portable barbecue grill to cook the burgers and hot dogs; there are conference tables borrowed from churches to hold the covered dishes everybody brings; and multiple coolers for soft drinks and beer show up as if by magic. We're primarily offering space."

"We'd need a couple of canopies or open tents for those who need to should stqy out of the sun and in case of rain. Chairs that won't sink into the yard, as well as six- or eight-person tables."

"I hope Beverly knows where we might find some of this," said Mark, somewhat hoping she couldn't and that he would be able to step up to provide a solution.

Mark peered at the Scrabble board and his letters. He was methodical in his strategy of the game as in the rest of his life. Making the most of the seven letters in his tray, he averaged more per play than Cathy did. She was a gambler, holding her blanks and S's in hopes of playing all seven letters in one go for the 50 point bonus.

They heard footsteps on the driveway. It was Officer Winston.

He saw them and called up. "Just thought you should know. Ray's out at the farm, sober enough to realize the family doesn't own this property anymore."

"I hope his memory is sufficiently blurry that he won't mix me up with the 'handyman' he met the other day."

"I wouldn't worry about that. "The policeman turned his hat around in his hands. "Oh, one more thing. Raymond seemed to think the July 4th event would be here. He probably was just hoping there would be one, as it's been harder each year to find new hosts."

"We have been . . . approached. And we've attended in the previous years—adding to the many bowls of potato salad—so we think we know what we would be getting into."

Officer Winston chuckled. "Yes, there's always too much of one dish and too little of others. But folks like to choose what they'll bring—independent minded, you might say."

Mark understood. He did wonder if he and Cathy were allowed to be "independent minded" or were they going to be restricted by traditions they would discover along the way. He said to Officer Winston, "We're considering it. Would we need to talk to you about security?"

"Security?" he chuckled. "You folks are new in town!"

Officer Winston was surveying their backyard. There was a flat area off the porch and deck, then the ground dipped down to a lower level. That slope marked an earlier riverbank. When the concrete bulkhead was put in farther out, the owners had fill dirt brought in behind it, but the lower yard would be very wet at certain seasons.

"There's one thing to consider . . ." Officer Winston observed.

"Yes?"

"Well, it's true of all the yards on Water Street, a constant underground shifting of mud and sand and water."

"Ah," Mark agreed. "Not exactly quicksand, but what's the water level here—one foot?"

"In your lower yard, that or less. But there have been stories about this spit of land between Water Street and the other side of Main. Next door, in fact, there's a drainage pipe that lets water move underground water from here to the public boat dock on Main and back. Helps prevent minor flooding."

Mark had heard water gurgling from the drain in his neighbor's side yard.

"Anyway, Matthew Jennings disappeared sometime in the 1930s—two houses down." Officer Winston gestured north. "Apparently, he went out during a heavy rain to check on the chicken coop they had."

"Flew the coop?"

"Hmm. Don't think so. He didn't show up anywhere else, and there was a bit of a sinkhole in that yard. Well, he had been drinking." Officer Winston spoke softly, "Now, don't quote me on this, but back in those days a lot of wives and mothers didn't approve of alcohol, even after though Prohibition was over. So, men stashed moonshine supplied by downriver stills in outbuildings—garages, tobacco sheds, chicken coops. And they'd go to 'work on something,' out of sight. Matt was one."

"So," said Cathy, "you're telling me he sank—or drank—out of sight?"

"Some did believe he planted himself, pint bottle in hand, in his own yard."

"So, we should worry about him rising out of the mud and

wanting to join the party?"

They all laughed. "I don't think that's likely, but I'd make sure folks are encouraged to stay on the high ground."

Mark concluded, "It is interesting, as if the land has a mind of its own."

He was thinking of how his home state of Missouri was famous for an underground identity—caves, shut-ins, springs, sink holes. It had taught him that landscape affects history. Vietnam's landscape, for instance—wetlands perfect for growing rice, mountains where indigenous people escaped the forces of history, ancient coastal cities dependent on and contributing to the sea.

After Winston left, Mark and Cathy continued the game until Mark heard the out-of-commission front doorbell ring. "What the . . . ?"

Cathy explained: "Bev fixed it." Mark suppressed his resentment. One of the attractions to retirement in an old house for him was home improvement projects.

He walked down the hall and opened the door to see a woman in a neat suit—white blouse, grey jacket, and slim skirt. She stepped back from the storm door, smiled, and offered Mark a business card. "Charlene Brown," she announced. "Your new neighbor."

Mark smiled back, "Mark Nelson. Step in and let me call my wife, Cathy."

He held open the door and gestured to what had originally been a parlor, with its separate door off the front porch and another to the screen porch. Family used to come in and out the main door whereas guests and visitors used the parlor door. Blacks, of course, went to the back.

"That's very kind." Charlene stepped in and surveyed what was now their library.

Walking down the hall, Mark glanced at the card and thought: "Uh-oh. A neighbor but also 'Real Estate Development Agent.'' What does this mean?"

He gave Cathy the card in such a way that she was encouraged to read it. She raised her eyebrows, gave him the card back, and preceded him down the hall.

They'd bought the Winston House from a Staffordshire agent, and he had explained there had been so little movement in local real estate market after 2008 that some agencies had shut down.

"Our new neighbor," Mark explained, and handed Cathy the card (again).

She glanced at it and said, "Nice to have you with us, Charlene. Please, sit. Are you on Water Street? Which house? They all have names associated with original owners."

"The Edwards House, just a block and a half north."

While Cathy praised the house and told her about close neighbors, Mark was wondering about Charlene's race. She sat straight in the wingback chair and crossed her legs. The Nelsons didn't use terms other than "white" or "person of color," but it seemed to him, this woman could be either dark-skinned one or light-skinned the other.

Cathy said, "We didn't know the house had been listed. The only owners we knew moved to Florida and were renting to folks down at Sandy Point Military Base." The little-known military institution was on the Albemarle Sound at the mouth of the Persimmon River, seven miles to the southeast. It had been a center for anti-submarine operations during World War II.

"Houses in some markets will sell without listing. And I'm a local girl come home, so I have my contacts." She smiled and shifted in her seat to face Cathy more directly. "After thirty years in the big city, I'm ready for slower pace and more space."

Cathy responded. "You've found it here. So, you're retiring or . . . ," she glanced at her card, " . . . beginning a new phase in your career?"

"I don't really need to work, but there may be opportunity opening up. That's why I'm making the rounds and introducing myself. Especially in . . . certain neighborhoods."

"Well, we're retired. I was in public relations, and . . ." he looked at Cathy.

"Hospital administration, a job that didn't exist when I started as a nurse years ago. We've owned this house for five years, but only moved here full-time from Virginia a year ago. Our children and their families are close enough for easy visits back and forth. And we're slowly being integrated into local affairs."

Charlene nodded. "Local affairs are part of why I'm knocking on doors. What do you hear about the replacement of our famous Short Bridge?"

Built in 1928, the draw bridge came in three blocks north of the Nelsons, where the river widens dramatically to form a kind of bay. It was short, but the road continued along a curving causeway to reach the town of Rockfall.

"The Short Bridge is a local landmark, but we know over the years it's suffered serious deterioration. It's not that safe now, and it's putting bad things in water."

"Right," agreed Charlene. "And we're going to want a say

in what's done with it. But today I'm just here to say 'hello' and hope to get to know you better in the weeks ahead."

She rose easily and they escorted her to the front door. When she'd left, Cathy told him about something he hadn't noticed about her. "Did you see her tattoo?"

"No. Where of what?"

"Well, one—there could be more—was, um, on the inside of her left leg just above the knee. An eagle with the words, 'Semper Fi.' It's not large, but not completely inconspicuous. I think she showed just me that tattoo. When she crossed her legs, she did it such a way that I saw it clearly, but you didn't have the angle."

"Ha! A Marine, then. Maybe she saw the Army star on the bumper of my car and wanted to . . . I don't know, declare her loyalties?"

Cathy raised her eyebrows. "Hmph!" she huffed.

Chapter Five: Nights

As they began the cocktail hour that evening, Cathy said to Mark, "One of the reasons I liked the idea of living here full-time was its stability. Not that I don't want to see some changes in such a small town, but a project like a new bridge can draw out opportunists."

"I understand," agreed Mark "There are a lot of routes a new road could go, not just following the path of the old. Some folks hope to profit by selling land they own, and there'll be a clever few who anticipate the potential value in currently unattractive property."

"I'm not drawing conclusions, but I do hope Charlene the Marine is doing what she said, working in the best interests of the whole town."

Mark handed her a glass of wine and poured himself a beer. "Charlene. . .that reminds me: are you thinking of getting a tattoo like hers?"

She raised her eyebrows. "Yes, but I think I'll go with the 'come hither' design, a curled finger"

"Um-hm. But returning to working in the best interests, Bruce and I were supposed to be showing how we were doing that in Vietnam, but I too often found opportunists at work."

"What I learned in college," said Cathy, "was that we were floundering by 1970 or so, basically hoping the Paris Peace Talks would result in a way of saving face."

"That would be accurate. Our officers sent us into the field to get stories and were willing to assume we were working hard, so long as we came back with something. Bruce and I, as I think I said, were audio correspondents, so we tried to do morale-boosting features where the sound gave a sense of being there."

"It wasn't dangerous?"

"It's true that traveling—hitchhiking on trucks and jeeps, using our press badges to catch rides on small planes and helicopters—could be risky. But I was never in real danger."

Cathy picked her favorites from the mixed nuts. She knew Mark felt each person should take what came randomly in a tablespoon; but she preferred, as she said, "freedom of choice."

"You came home safely."

He took a spoonful of nuts. "Yes, but Bruce saw assignment to Vietnam as an opportunity. Within a few months of being there he was getting friends back home to send him American currency (illegal but highly valuable on the black market) and was recruiting guys going on R & R in Tokyo, Bangkok, and Sydney to bring back electronic equipment he could sell to GIs in the bush."

"Illegal? Or just skirting official policy?"

"A little of both. But there were NCO's—non-commissioned officers—who knew what he was up to. Sergeant-Major West called him in one day. The conversation went something like this." Mark made his voice lower and raspy. 'PFC Badass,' [Bruce's real name was Backus.] 'we need to have us a talk. Tell me about these so-called leads you're finding.'"

"Bruce could generally blow smoke up anyone's behind, but West had been in for 28 years and knew bullshit when he heard it. He came around his desk stood nose-to-nose with his E-4. 'Explain that chopper scout scheme again.'"

Mark said that Bruce was going to be a second observer on a Loach. "Loach" was the nickname for the "light observation helicopters" being put to increasing use in the mountainous regions. The pilots of these small choppers, fearless, flew just over the treetops and scouted out the enemy.

Mark looked out at the river and, it seemed to Cathy, saw the landscape of Vietnam in 1970. He recounted what happened almost as if she wasn't there to hear.

Bruce told Sarge that he'd let the tape recorder run, record the conversation of pilot and gunner while he took photos.

But West was right back at him. "Shit, Badass," he said. "I know what Loaches do, finding LZs for our guys and pinpointing enemy locations."

The small choppers couldn't fly fast enough to escape enemy fire. And they didn't carry weapons that made them a meaningful threat. West knew this was risky verging on foolish.

Bruce had made the contacts for his Loach mission, however, and the assignment was approved. He did two trial runs to test has equipment. He was taking the place of a gunner who sometimes rode out on missions.

Every time Bruce came back to the base he carried a pocketful of 35 mm film. He had been a skilled photographer in civilian life and planned to produce a photo album that would show war's reality. He mailed negatives and prints back to a brother in Denver without ever showing them to their commander. It was, of course, all official government property, but he assumed no one would notice the acts of one man in a force of half a million.

Bruce developed his film in the unit's lab. Technically, he wasn't allowed to use the facility, especially because the half a dozen unit photographers were busy there all day. But not at night. So, Bruce started staying in and processing film through until the morning.

That led to his habit of napping during the day in the broadcast studio's sound booth, using the equipment to play favorite songs from home: "We Gotta' Get Out of this Place," "Sitting on the Dock of the Bay," "Leaving on a Jet Plane." He was out of sight below the double thick glass-paned window, and the soundproofing carpet on the floor was a satisfactory mattress. He used his equipment bag as a pillow.

Long Binh was the site of Army Headquarters (US-ARV-HQ) in-country, so there was a separate compound to house the generals. It wasn't unusual to see two, three, or more marching through the complex to a strategy session or mission review. New arrivals often got the tour of the facility and were sometimes curious about the sound studio.

Mark generally turned on the red "Recording" light in the hall so he could work uninterrupted. It was not lit one morning, though; and when Mark heard a rap on the door, he opened it without thinking. Then he snapped to attention and snapped off a salute. "Sirs."

Mark's CO, a colonel, said, "We're escorting these new officers through the facility, Specialist. Explain what we have here."

"Yes, sir. State-of-the-art, reel-to-reel machines," he said, turning to wave at the two consoles, each as big as a refrigerator. "Ampex, best there is."

They weren't, but the brass always wanted to think they were. "We have a cabinet full of cassette recorders to take into the field. Glad to play you some of our features, Sir."

Mark was trying to keep them from examining the sound booth. But the big microphone on its boom and the little ones on the counter visible through the window always drew the attention of visitors.

"This where the announcer sits?" asked one of the generals, gesturing.

"Yes, Sir. But you know, sir, it's really the guy out here," he pointed back to the control deck with its circular sound dials and slide control panel, "who make it all happen. You see, the soundtrack is raw, but it gets filtered and shaded . . . " He spun some knobs and pushed buttons to light up dials.

"Step in here, Sir" said Colonel Charles, smiling, "and Nelson there will record you for prosperity. You can send a message home to your family." He swung open the sound booth door.

And there was Bruce flat on his back.

Charles glared at Mark. "What's this, Specialist?"

"Ah, yes, . . . um, Specialist Backus, Sir. He gets so caught up in a story that he sometimes stays late to work on it and then sleeps in. It's almost as if he's on the night shift." He chuckled as if he'd made a good joke.

Colonel Charles slammed the door (though, so well insulated, it didn't make a sound).

Mark tried to keep up his chatter. "Sirs, he's been out on scout helicopters, doing a feature on one of the most dangerous missions we've undertaken in my time here. They fly low and depend on speed to escape enemy fire. Can't get him to take a break, even though he's scheduled to fly again tomorrow."

Charles shepherded the generals back into the hall. "Next, where our Stars and Stripes reporters work, just like the press rooms you see in the movies." The glare he sent Mark meant he would be back without the brass.

After the Colonel chewed them both out about the sound booth incident, Bruce showed up back at Long Binh less and less. And he didn't bring back stories. Then word came in: he and the Loach pilot had been blown out of the sky somewhere up in the Central Highlands. The bodies were never found.

Cathy took a final sip of wine. "I have a funny feeling that once you were home, you worried that the next door you opened would reveal Bruce in the same position the generals had found him, stretched out flat on the floor—protecting our freedom."

Mark appreciated--but at the same time resented--his wife's ability to understand him and his past so well.

Recalling how divisive the Vietnam War had been, he wondered if the nation today was more capable of unity. If he and Cathy were having trouble staying on the same page about hosting the July 4 celebration, could he ask more of the larger community? He would have to try harder to match her sense of commitment to the project—and to their marriage.

Chapter Six: Halves

"Good news!" called Anne-Harriet, their across-the-street neighbor, as Cathy and Mark, out for morning exercise, walked past. "The Whole Whole Van is in town again. Douglas, the baker, makes the best."

"Whole donuts, I take it," said Cathy, "rather than donut holes."

Anne-Harriet laughed and pointed a finger at her. "It's not only that his donuts aren't just holes, his bakery is housed in a . .   what do you call it? Oh, a teardrop trailer, that's it. He pulls it behind a restored VW Beetle. Each is a semi-circle, and together they make a whole donut-shape."

Mark asked, "So, his is a traveling business, a gypsy caravan of one."

"That's right. He drives from Florida to Massachusetts in early summer every year and goes back in late fall, along the way baking and selling the most delicious cider donuts to pay for gas and supplies. He's an . . . interesting . . . character."

Back in their house Mark made a mental note about the stability and fluidity of social structures in Staffordshire: these old-timers stayed put, but an entire business, a donut factory, came and went up and down the coast. It was sort of like what

Officer Winston explained—the earth shifting in their yards as water comes and goes beneath.

Cathy gestured toward the highway that crossed the Persimmon River half a mile out. "I'm not sure there's a pot of gold over there, but apparently there is a box of golden donuts for me at the end of the bridge. Be sure to bring enough for Anne-Harriet, too."

Mark agreed. "They'd better have a helpful slogan, or I return to Bojangles."

"That would hardly be the end of the world," she laughed.

He didn't at first see a slogan on the donut-colored Whole Donut Van because he approached from the side, where a window shutter dropped down to make a sales shelf. Douglas took orders on the left side of the window, passed out boxes in the center, and collected money (using an old-fashioned cash register that went "ka-ching") in the right third of the window. Before he left, Mark did find an intriguing slogan on the back of the teardrop trailer.

There was a line of a dozen customers in front of Mark, confirming the operation's popularity. He squinted at the list of products and prices on a sign hanging from two hooks to the left of the window.

"I had never heard of 'cider donuts,'" noted a voice from the line extending behind Mark. "But I have to admit, even though it's some kind of Northern concoction, they're pretty damn good, don't you think?"

Mark turned to see a man he guessed to be a senior senior (rather than a junior one) wearing hunting clothes and a New York Yankee's baseball cap. "Well," he admitted, "this is my first time, so I'll have to reserve judgment. But you recommend them?"

"Sure do, young man. Especially, when you're planning to hire a group of guys to help set up the July 4 picnic, which, I understand, you'll be doing."

"Excuse me? I don't know for sure that my wife and I are hosting, and, if we do, we won't need a crew."

The man grinned and extended a hand. "Thomas Beard. That's what they all say, but, in the end, you'll need half a dozen, at least. Your children, grandchildren, or in-laws coming to help?"

Shaking Thomas Beard's hand, Mark realized it was covered with scars. He looked up into this face and saw scars there, too. Only patches of his eyebrows remained.

"Hi, Thomas. Mark Nelson. It's . . . uh . . . unlikely at this point."

They'd brought up to both families the prospect of helping the annual block party, but Louis's and Mary's children had customary events to attend on the holiday. Mark wondered if he could use that to back away from the commitment.

There had always been some friction related to change in their marriage. Cathy seemed never to feel the anxiety he did at taking on new friends, extra responsibilities, unexpected opportunities. Mark worried that aging could be the force that undermined their future together.

The Whole Donuts line had been moving steadily all this time, and Mark realized he should scan the menu again to make his choice.

"Get a dozen of the plain for a starter," Thomas recommended. "Later, try the ones with powdered sugar. Your workers will like a mix."

Thomas turned his head to scan the line behind him, and Mark noticed that his neck was also scarred. He had to assume that this man had been badly injured in a fire at some time in his past.

"Okay. Where did you learn we were . . . that there would be a July 4 party? You live in the neighborhood?"

"Naw, Sonny. I do the fireworks. And I get paid more than donuts, I hope you understand. But I'll come by the house, and you and the missus can go over what you want. I run down to Over the Line every year, and I can get you anything—though I reserve the right to --improvise a bit myself, having been 'Fireworks Tom' for over over thirty years." Over the Line was a sprawling truck stop--restaurant--gift shop--motel-- fireworks market just south of the North Carolina-South Carolina border.

Thomas continued, "There's your standard firecrackers, sparklers, poppers and snakes, roman candles, flying fish—that's a good one for down here 'cause I set them off in my boat out in the river—comets, aerial repeaters, willows, and—now I don't tell the ladies the name of this one—bat and balls."

"Give me a dozen of the regular," Mark told Douglas.

To this point Mark had only seen a large man moving from a counter covered in flour to a skillet on a single electric burner to a deep fryer to the window. Now he saw that this was a very large, muscular, bald man with pale eyebrows and big smile. When he paused in his work, he crossed his arms in front of a white T-shirt and apron. It occurred to Mark that he resembled the figure on a Mr. Clean bottle and recalled that the original model for that image was thought to be a United States Navy sailor.

"$12.00 even, my friend. That's a dozen plus two of my choice, no extra charge."

Mark handed him a ten and two ones. Two extra donuts? Why was it everyone he dealt with around here felt free to alter expected exchanges whenever it suited them? Perhaps he liked order and convention too much.

He would have liked to chat about the man's mobile operation, but the line of customers snaked out behind him was growing, and Douglas was baking, boxing, and selling at a rapid pace. So, Mark resolved to come back at a less busy hour. He wandered around the factory, curious about the unusual vehicle.

He also processed disfigurements he saw on Douglas' arms, neck, and face. Working with a deep fat fryer in a cramped mobile van likely accounted for his appearance. Mark hadn't been able to view more, but he hoped the baker's summer attire was not shorts and sandals.

He knew chefs and kitchen workers suffered many injuries, which is why most don't stay in their roles too long. Cuts by sharp knives, back strains from lifting large pots heavy with liquids, foot injuries coming with long hours on concrete floors, bones broken by slips and wet surfaces, and burns. They are always around frying pans, boiling water/sauces, and open flames. He wondered what would follow being a doughnut baker in Douglas' career.

It was not hard to see Thomas Beard's scarred arms and face were also connected to his profession. Fireworks were the major Fourth of July attractions for the boys he'd grown up with in a small Missouri town. All those aged seven and older were turned loose with the bag of fireworks they'd paid for with their allowances. Injuries inevitably occurred.

The most potent explosives were the cherry bombs (red spheres with a thick green fuse sticking out like an umbilical cord) and the salutes (silver cylinders with a silver fuse in the middle of one side). But individual firecrackers (usually in packs of sixteen) were standard in every boy's arsenal, as were lady fingers (small firecrackers stitched together so they went off like a tiny machine gun)

Mark tired of the whole business when he was eleven or twelve, suddenly finding no joy in bang after bang after bang. He gave away what was left of his stash, And Donny Parker, two years younger, subsequently used some of the lady fingers to burn a patch of fur off his dog. The expression "WTF?" was not current then, but it applied.

In the end, Mark found a bumper sticker he liked on the traveling bakery van. It said, "No try, just do," which alluded, he assumed, to Yoda's wisdom in Star Wars. Still, the dictum appealed to him, and he would see if Cathy might consider it rule number two, after 'No Negativity,' for the summer.

Whether she approved of its poetic structure—the two "o" sounds and the two balanced phrases—or simply fell in love with cider donuts was not clear. But the injunction was adopted for additional guidance in their summer project.

Chapter Seven: Fire

Among of the attractions of Staffordshire for the Nelsons were sunrises and sunsets. The view to the east from Water Street was especially impressive at both dusk and dawn. On clear mornings they could watch the sun come up across the river and the flat land beyond: first a slim rim of a red disk; then the one quarter, half, three-quarter circle, and finally full circle.

If there was fog rising off the river or low clouds in the east, a mix of yellow, red, and orange blended with the blue sky and went through phases of shifting color and shape. The Nelsons' 90-year-old neighbor Vickie said she'd never seen the same sunrise twice.

Sunsets were spectacular in their own right because the sun dropping in the West cast horizontal rays across the flat fields and lit up the bridge crossing the river half a mile out and parallel to Water Street. The long structure changed color as it was lit up—silver (the metal) turned to yellow, orange, gold.

A regular group of neighborhood seniors celebrated the sunset while sitting out on Anne-Harriet's side porch across the street from the Nelsons.

"Come on up here, young people," called their neighbor as Cathy and Mark walked past a few days after the donut excursion. Of course, they loved the flattery (that they were "young people"); but Anne-Harriet, like many on Water Street, was in her nineties.

The "young people" walked and biked regularly around town, and they were still hoping to find a tennis league. They'd played wherever they were throughout their marriage.

Anne-Harriet introduced them to Patrick Martin, retired paper mill manager, and his wife, Vickie, retired school teacher. They lived four houses north. Also there, were the Pattersons, Carl, a retired hydraulics engineer, and his wife, Klara, a native of Denmark. They lived across the street two houses south.

When Cathy and Mark had fixed themselves drinks, Anne-Harriet informed them, "Now, I have some advice for you two about July 4, but it will have to wait until I finish telling what happened to me a few days ago--Wednesday, I guess it was. I was sitting in Darlene's. You know Darlene's," she looked at Cathy, "the beauty parlor over on Market Street?"

She didn't stop for a response. "I was under the dryer, had the curlers in, and this woman I don't know walks in."

The guests had grown up together in or around Hartford during the Depression, been through the war together, and continued the fine old Southern tradition of socializing regularly for over six decades. Anne-Harriet's husband, a retired Social Security executive, had passed away twenty years ago. She'd always been a good storyteller, and now, living alone, she was even more ready to narrate.

"Well, this woman was moving slowly--she was a large woman--and she groaned and grunted all the way to a chair. Of course, since Sharlene put those two extra chairs in there, we all have to navigate around the obstacles." Sharlene was Darlene's daughter, who inherited the business thirty years ago and kept the shop's name.

"Even under the dryer," Anne-Harriet went on, "I could hear her talking. I couldn't make out much with the noise of the machine, but I thought she was going on and on about 'the chickens.'"

"Was Martha Jane working that day?" interrupted Klara. Martha Jane was her regular hairdresser, confidante to more town secrets that anyone except Sharon, the town clerk.

"She was. And that's who took this lady." She held up her glass." Carl, be a dear." He filled her glass with Chardonnay. As he took the bottle from the patio tea table, he winked at Klara. The side porch was Queen Anne-Harriet's kingdom.

"By the way, I almost forgot. While I was there, I heard Regina Wilson is in rehab again. If she keeps falling down, we're going to lose her, too."

When Anne-Harriet said "lose her," she didn't mean their friend was going to die, only that yet another bridge partner, participant at church suppers, and Daughter of the American Revolution would be taken out of circulation. To this group going to the nursing home on Market Street, even into the assisted care section, was not just a loss of freedom, but the end of a meaningful life.

Anne-Harriet continued. "After a while it was time for me to get out from under the dryer, and that woman was still talking. I didn't know her and had no idea why she was making all that fuss, but she told Martha Jane, 'I'm soooo tired today, just plumb worn out after all that. My feet hurt, and my back aches, and my legs feel like dead tree stumps.' I mean, she carried on the whole time her hair was being done and kept on going as I was getting brushed out and ready to go."

Patrick objected. "Some people still work hard, you know. Of course, we don't have any factories in town that hire people for labor anymore, and the farming's all done by machines. But maybe she has a few acres she works with her family."

His own family had suffered when the last of Staffordshire's plants closed in 1941. He'd joined the Army in part to make a new start. That didn't happen until he'd spent three years in Asia with his fellow Army engineers.

"She could be cleaning houses out at the Colony. Was she black?" asked Carl. The gated development had grown rapidly in the 1990s, creating a new group of elite residents who generally kept to themselves but did hire landscapers, housecleaners, and repair personnel. Their exclusivity irritated old-timers like this group, the elite of established families.

"I think she might be related to the Blackburns," mused Anne-Harriet. "She sure did look like them."

Carl said, "I was there looking in on Bobby Winston just the other day." Mark would learn that this Winston was the uncle of their garage guest. He and Carl enlisted together in

1942. They'd gone from Normandy to Berlin.

"What are the rooms like at that rehab place?" asked Anne-Harriet. She'd made a point of not going to the center, even to visit friends.

Carl explained. "They have them two to a room, and the rooms are small. It looks like they're trying to use every corner of the old house. And the therapy rooms are crammed with machines, and elevator music is everywhere. I truly wonder if all the openings are big enough for wheelchairs." They'd all made their children measure their doors. fearful of being told one day that they couldn't stay in their homes. The prospect of losing their independence was frightening.

Magnolia Rest, the nursing home, had bought the old Franklin Boarding House on South Main Street and turned it into a rehabilitation facility. They divided the already modest rooms into smaller units, and the local aging population was filling them quickly.

"How did you find a place to park?" asked Anne-Harriet. "There's no room in their lot, and Ace Hardware has leased the town spaces in front for their customers."

Staffordshire had been skipped over by the Walmart's and Lowe's, which had stores in Harbor City to the north and Newtown to the south. But the influx of retirees from farther up the East Coast and a growing number of commuters who drove daily to the Norfolk area had made this tiny town seem crowded. Because of the way the river wound around it, there was no room for expansion of the old neighborhoods.

"Anyway," said Anne-Harriet loudly to regain the group's attention. "As I listened to this woman complain about the chickens, I tried to figure out how they'd had made her so tired. We all had chickens on the farm and in the backyards here in town."

"That's true," agreed Patrick. "You make sure they've got enough feed and water, the rest of the time they take care of themselves."

Anne-Harriet huffed, "We ought to keep a few more of the outsiders out, if you ask me." She waved a hand at the junior seniors. "Not you two. You fit right in, and your house has always been here. And that brings me to pieces of advice I have about the summer celebration."

Mark smiled. "Well, we haven't really decided, but we're certainly taking any advice just in case."

"Okay. If you take it on, be advised that you have to let Pastor Baldwin bless the meal." He was the minister at Staffordshire Baptist. "He does live on Water Street, so he's automatically invited. But . . . he seems a sensitive type, and he's not been a minister that long."

"That's less either of us would have to say," agreed Mark. "So, check."

"Also: even though the Simpsons live on Water Street and technically should be included, you have to exclude them."

"The reason . . . ," wondered Cathy.

"Their granddaughter always visits over holiday, and she is . . . um, a free spirit who believes in free love. She'll be luring young men and old into your garage or your upstairs bedrooms or an empty bathroom and accepting contributions to her 'college fund.'" (She used finger quotes).

Chapter Eight. Meat

"Sooo, anyway," Anne-Harriet resumed. "The chicken lady, this Miss or Mrs. Blackburn (maybe), got up to leave, and all of a sudden I remembered I'd seen her before, right there in Darlene's. It must have been the previous month, maybe the one before that."

"Ah, a regular customer, then."

"I guess so, though this Wednesday time might be new for her."

Vickie chuckled. "Yes, you've been going every third Wednesday for over forty years, and you'd have noticed before."

"Anyway, then I recalled she'd said the same things that other time, about how tired she was, her legs hurting and so on. Now, she's a large woman, a very large woman, and her weight alone might affect her legs. She didn't mention chickens the other time that I remember, but it was *déjà vu* for me."

"And this time you asked her?"

"And she said, she'd been 'walking the chickens' all day and now was 'plumb wore out.'"

Mark asked, "'Walking the chickens,' though? Does that mean she puts them on leashes and parades them through town?"

"I know what it means," said Patrick. "But you go ahead," he gestured to Anne-Harriet, aware that she wanted to finish the story herself.

"It's one of those giant chicken houses, thousands of square feet, and the birds are so thick in there they cover the floor, beak to tail, if you see what I mean."

"Well, not beak to tail, as they're 'de-beaked' early," said Patrick. "The 'farmers'--if I can use the term loosely--slice off their beaks so they won't peck each other to death."

Cathy said, "I understand chickens aren't the smartest animals, but cooped up like that, I can see why they'd go stir crazy."

Mark glanced at Cathy. Sometimes he mocked how women gossiped, referring to them as "old hens" and alluding to what he claimed was legendary chicken stupidity. She would retaliate now and then with references to men as billy goats.

Patrick explained, "They're sociable animals, chickens are, living in groups of maybe thirty. They have a hierarchy, and they know each other. They share the same activities like dust bathing and can communicate with chirps and crowing."

Vickie confirmed. "'Broiler-chicken factories,' they call those giant sheds. Tens of thousands of birds under one roof, not a square foot of space for each bird. They can't do what their ancestors have done since the beginning of time: roam, scratch in the dirt, socialize. Because of the crowding, they end up fighting each other even with no beaks."

Anne-Harriet frowned. "That's certainly not a good thing, but around here we can still get beef and chicken at the butcher on the other side of the bridge. And that's not why I'm telling this anyway . . . or at least, not exactly."

"Go on, please," said Mark, glancing at Cathy. While they didn't eat red meat, neither had given up chicken, which they purchased at the grocery store and which came no doubt from a "broiler factory."

"So, I did ask this woman--still not knowing her name--I asked her how chickens had made her so tired."

"Maybe she walks them on a treadmill," ventured Cathy. "But then she could just stand there and watch them."

"Hello, Reverend," said Anne-Harriet. And everyone turned to greet James Baldwin, the Staffordshire Methodist church minister, who was sauntering down the sidewalk. "Come join us for a spell. I'm telling a good story, which you cannot use in a sermon." She pointed a finger at him with the word "not."

The minister smiled in agreement, helped himself to a beer from the cold box beside the tea table, and settled in a canvas yard chair. He seemed to be somewhere in his 50's, younger than the "junior seniors." Cathy noted that his clothes fit rather tightly, as if he'd recently put on weight/

"Well, here's what the chicken-walker said," Anne-Harriet went on after filling James in on the situation, "'It's walking 'em, Ma'am,' the lady explained. 'The owner wants someone to walk through them every hour or so, to keep them active, I guess.'"

"Doesn't seem like a hard job." Mark commented. "I wonder if there are a crew of walkers taking day and night shifts. Poor birds would never be free to rest."

Anne-Harriet chuckled. "I just couldn't get the picture out of my head of this, well, very large woman waltzing across a chicken house with little birds fluttering into the air all around her like flowers at the prom."

Patrick sighed. "The idea is to stir them up, so the weaker ones aren't left on the bottom. But they still find hundreds dead each day as they go through the chick stage." He had turned down several offers to convert the family wheat/corn/

soybean/cotton fields to chicken broiler factories.

"It's not a floor either," noted Carl. "It's a wire mesh. Their feet can get caught in the wire. When they get bigger, their weight will leave crisscross marks. But, the way they're fed, the birds reach maturity quickly;—if you call simply as plump as they can get them 'mature'."

Vickie added. "They pack them in crates, stack the crates on a flatbed, carry them off to the slaughterhouse. You get behind one on the road, and it looks like a wall of cotton, they've smashed them in so tight. Something like 8,000 birds an hour get . . . are slaughtered."

Anne-Harriet frowned. "Well, you've certainly put a sad ending to what was supposed to be a funny story about . . . about what goes on in the modern world. But," she sighed, "it may be time here on Water Street to conclude the afternoon's discussion."

There was an immediate rising, gathering of purses, and straightening of chairs. After the customary thanks and promises to return soon, the group was on their way.

On the sidewalk Reverend Baldwin spoke to Mark and Cathy, "I hear you'll be hosting July Fourth this year. Good for you."

"Well, . . ."

"Here's a piece of advice: any extra things you need, go out to Sal's Junk Shop on Wharf Street by the abandoned shopping center. She sells on consignment but ends up with unclaimed items she'll give you a good price on or loan out."

They promised to keep that in mind.

When they were back in their house, Cathy and Mark tried

to take in what Anne-Harriet asserted about a college age girl finding marks at a neighborhood party. "Surely that was hyperbole, said Cathy, "like Anne-Harriet's chickens moving around as if they were live cotton balls."

Mark nodded. "But we might want see if we can get confirmation."

"Yes. I'm also curious about the Baptist minister. He had on a wedding band, but no one has mentioned a wife."

"Sounds like a topic for Darlene's."

"Beverly—or our garage guest—probably knows, as well as whether or not the college fund scheme is real."

"Good point," agreed Mary. "She's coming tomorrow to do some yard work and see what might be done with our cypress knees."

The Nelsons' lower yard was soft and wet, especially after rain. The cypress knees sent roots out laterally, which made the trees able to withstand strong winds. But from those large horizontal roots thick vertical roots spring up vertically, most just a few inches tall, but some get several feet high. Specialists are not sure of their purpose: perhaps they provide mechanical support for the large heavy trees; maybe they collect oxygen.

Whatever their function, the knees make mowing with a conventional lawn mower difficult. Some of his neighbors have a ritual chain saw removal of the stumps every spring, giving more space for grass; others let their riding mowers cut them with each pass. The trees don't seem to suffer. But Cathy thinks they must serve some purpose, and she's asked Mark to leave them.

He'd mapped a route around the worst of them, but he

wondered if he shouldn't let the yard alone. Native plants would take over and need less care. He'd be free to do other things.

He compared cypress knees to individuals in every family and neighborhood who stick up, get in the way, but serve no clear purpose. He kind of liked his garage guest, though, so he wasn't labeling him a tree knee. And he felt he could work with Fireworks Tom. The Simpson woman, however, might be taking up space that should be open.

Chapter Nine: Soundings

Mark later told Cathy, "You need to ask Anne-Harriet if fireworks are essential for the 4th. You know I've become less comfortable with them over the years."

"Yes, like many veterans, you don't need any more explosions of sound and light. I know that our occasional downriver fireworks are not pleasurable background noise for you."

Sandy Point Military Base was seven miles to the southeast, a restricted facility whose exact purpose was unknown. Most locals believed it was run by the CIA and provided a place to test experimental weapons and space to practice clandestine operations. It had shorelines on both the Persimmon River and the Albemarle Sound; and it was rumored that mock campaigns had been staged there by Navy, Marine, and Army forces.

Rumors circulated in 2011 and later than a model of Osama Bin Laden's compound had been constructed at Sandy Point and that it was one of several locations used to work out the final plan of assault. Of course, such stories were connected to other bases, as well. But the sense that a phase of such a momentous operation in the nation's history had occurred in the Staffordshire area created an aura of importance for the community.

Mark didn't like the secrecy of Sandy Point, believing it gave the military too much freedom to experiment, develop, and test weapons that would appeal to hawkish politicians. And, given free rein to pursue vague outcomes, too many contractors exploded budgets (not enemy capability) with cost overruns.

On occasional days in all seasons explosions could be heard coming from the base, especially when there was an east wind. Did it signify there were more training exercises, new weapon designs, variations in the shape of American military action in some distant part of the globe? Were they precursors to another "Shock and Awe" operation in a rogue country? No one could say, but what troubled Mark and some other veterans were echoes of their past experiences in war zones.

While the world watched video of the aerial assault on Iraq in 2003 as a fireworks display, veterans had a clearer picture of what was happening on the ground. Mark had recalled a neighbor back in their Virginia home joking about "shock and awe" when boiling lobsters.

He'd not been pleased to watch the wiggling live creatures dropped headfirst into boiling water, even though he was assured they didn't feel a thing--death was so quick, and they had primitive nervous systems anyway.

"Hear that?" the man in charge said to him, cocking his ear over the boiling water. Mark leaned closer and picked up a high-pitched sound, as if the lobsters were crying. He looked up, shocked.

But the cook laughed. "That's just gas coming through their shells, man. Sounds like a baby, though, don't it?"

"There's no pain?"

"Not unless you let them get your fingers with their pincers or spill the water on your privates!"

He recalled stepping out of a jet plane onto the steaming dark tarmac at Cam Rahn Bay Air Force Base. He was amazed he didn't melt on the spot. Once home he was grateful his later experiences in Vietnam had left no visible scars.

"So," Cathy told him, "Beverly wants to know if you'd like the garage shaped up? She says there are some rotting pieces of siding, and the vertical posts need shoring up."

While vinyl siding had been put on the house at some point, the garage still had its original hardwood siding. He had scraped and painting bad spots easily visible from Water Street, but he knew more should be done, especially if they were going to utilize the building on the 4th.

Still, this was a project he preferred to take on himself, so he said, "Let's ask her for an estimate and see what she thinks could be done . . . for a limited amount of money and in time for the celebration."

Cathy's father had had an extension added to his garage in Virginia Beach, creating a study with a record player, radio, small refrigerator, and shelves where he stored his collection of toy mechanical banks. After retirement, he entertained friends with songs from the '40s played on vinyl records and tales from all decades embellished by his imagination.

Other houses on Water Street had restored and new outbuildings.

Mark's father was not a collector and was not good at small talk. A professor of astronomy at a small Midwestern university, his mind was, Mark's mother always told him, in the sky. He had a canvas folding chair he opened in the front of the garage and would sit there on weekends smoking his pipe and contemplating the observable heavens.

Mark had thought, if he had time and could clear out the garage, he would build wooden sailboats there. It was a romantic notion, he knew, that grew out of childhood dreams; but he did manage to construct a 12-foot dinghy. He was inspired by his senior senior neighbor, Patrick.

His 90-year-old fiend had his 22-foot, gaff-rigged sailboat moored fifty yards offshore. He rowed out from his dock on a wooden skiff, climbed aboard, and took it down the river. Vickie would not let him go alone anymore, so several times in the past Mark had been an untrained first mate.

Still, Mark was agile enough and eager enough that he could do what the skipper needed. He was not allowed to raise mainsail or jib, but at times he was put at the rudder and that gave Patrick opportunities to make adjustments on other parts of the boat.

One day, Patrick said, "Take the tiller for me, would you? I want to just stretch out here for a bit of rest." He lay on his back on the starboard bench and pulled the brim of his bucket sun hat down over his eyes.

Uneasily, Mark asked, "And, um, my orders, Captain?"

"Just hold it steady. With this wind we should stay right in the middle of the river."

Mark knew only that when he pulled the tiller to the right (starboard), the boat moved to the left (port); and vice versa. But he assumed this boating veteran wouldn't put them in danger. Still, when the wind picked up, there was a pull on the tiller, and Mark tightened his grip to hold it still.

Then sounds came from Sandy Point, now about three miles ahead of them, a low rumbling like distant thunder. Without lifting his hat Patrick said, "Testing today."

"Ah. Not in our direction, I assume."

Patrick chuckled. "No, sounds to me that could be under ground or underwater, the muffled nature of it."

"I guess you get used to it the longer you're here. Still, it's bit disconcerting, I think, not to know what they're up to."

Patrick sat up. "When I was building roads in Burma during, the war, we heard shelling and bombing every day. And the guys who'd been there for a good while could tell you what the explosions meant—us or the Japanese, advancing or retreating, stationary."

"You were an engineer, right? So, you weren't heading out to engage the enemy on a regular basis."

"Right, though if they got close, I did my duties like any soldier."

Mark nodded. "I was the same as a correspondent in Vietnam. I wasn't a combat soldier, but traveling to cover stories could take me to contested areas. Pulling regular guard duty at night, I could see lights and hear sounds from distant firefights—cobra gunshots raining down fire on enemy positions with their mini-guns. The seasoned veterans could interpret the sounds from miles away—ambush, counterattack, routine shelling of known positions."

"You get used to Sandy Point sounds the same way." He chuckled again. "I might give you some extra advice about listening to sounds in town as well as out on the river."

"I guess I'd better start paying more attention to people like Raymond Winston, who showed up one morning last week in my garage."

"Ray can surprise you with what he knows. And this is a typical small town, and word travels fast. To a newcomer like you, without knowing the history of the place, some of it might seem like code." He saved his eyes. "We're about as far downriver as we need to be today. Prepare to come about."

Of course, Mark didn't do anything to assist in coming about except turn the tiller over to the captain and prepare to duck when they changed tact. He had to be low to avoid getting clobbered by the boom swinging across the boat as the sails took the wind from the other side. Careless solo sailors had been knocked unconscious and lost control of their boat.

When Patrick had tied off the jib and the mainsail, he offered one more piece of advice. "Now, on the 4th of July thing: I recommend Cathy have an extra appointment or two a Darlene's. You know, to listen to the chatter for distant, um, gunfire."

Chapter Ten: Chickens

Back from her first visit to Darlene's, Cathy announced, "I'm officially part of the community, but on probation. And I can tell you some of what I learned today!"

"I'm ready to hear," offered Mark, "but don't reveal anything a man is not supposed to know." He was pleased not to see a drastic difference in her hair.

They were in the kitchen/family room preparing dinner for the same people (minus the minister) who'd been at Anne-Harriet's earlier in the week. It was more of their getting known and knowing their neighbors as they moved toward the 4th.

"The first thing," said Cathy, "is that there used to be a grass tennis court between Patrick and Vickie's house and the one next door. I bet she played there as a child. I learned that she was quite an athlete."

Mark said, "I wish it was still there!" He and Cathy loved grass and clay, but almost always had to play on hard courts.

"The second thing I learned is that the town is finally getting the courage to confront out-of-town property owners who've let houses sit empty and decay."

"The revitalization idea," said Mark. "That would be good for all of us property owners who have improved these old homes."

"As I understood it," Cathy continued, "the town council is going to demand back taxes in some cases and insist on repairs to bring structures up to code."

Mark nodded. "Both overdue gestures, I'm sure. Excuse me a minute. I need to step outside and check the grill."

Mark liked to use charcoal rather than gas, though it made exact timing in cooking problematic. Today he would do chicken breasts and salmon filets.

When he returned, giving a thumbs up sign to Cathy, she continued the story from Darlene's. "Two years ago, the town put in a 'historic walking path' they hoped would make the town more attractive. But the only ones who tour it come from the Colony, and they cluck their tongues at the places in need of repair."

Mark frowned. "So, passersby we don't recognize are likely be our effete neighbors looking at old homes as if we're all residents of a museum."

"Anne-Harriet and Vickie find it offensive." She cocked her head. "Get the door, will you. I'm putting in the squash casserole." Again, he felt a twinge of resentment that Bev had repaired the doorbell.

Vickie had grown up in what was now officially designated "The Winston House" by the historical society. She (a Winston before marriage only distantly related to Raymond) and her husband had lived in western Virginia for thirty-five years after the war before returning and building on a family lot three doors up on Water Street

Vickie's sister-in-law, Irene, had inherited the old home. When she passed away, the family decided to sell it rather than undertake needed repairs and upgrades.

Cathy and Mark first saw the house before all belongings had been removed. The floors of the upstairs bedrooms were covered with stacks of old magazines, newspapers, and boxes—some with unopened appliances purchased by credit card. Both mother and son had been hoarders. As they toured, Mark whispered to Cathy, "Southern Gothic."

Once their guests were settled in the family room, Anne-Harriet complimented their hosts on keeping the spirit of the old home. Klara added, "There's just so much space in these old homes; it's wonderful you've kept it open—not like Magnolia Rest and the rehab center."

Carl agreed. "When there's no family member in the area, they don't get the best treatment. It's a shame, really."

Patrick added, "They don't have enough staff, I think. You walk down the hall there, and you hear people calling out. 'Nurse, nurse!' or 'Help me,' or 'I need to go to bed now.'

I've gone in a few rooms now and then, no idea who's there. And I tell you what, they're happy to see me."

Anne-Harriet clucked. "You have to keep up if you're ever in one of those places. Do your crossword puzzles, keep reading, play bridge. If your mind isn't challenged, it atrophies just like any other muscle--your legs, for instance, when you don't walk enough."

Vickie sighed. "But it's hard, you know. Patrick now, he's always working in the yard or attending Rotary or off to Bible study. I'm not so mobile, and, if I don't watch out, I'll spend whole days sitting in my favorite chair reading and just looking out at the water."

Mark excused himself to tend to the grill, musing over the prospects these new friends were facing and their efforts to stay active as they aged. Carl still tended two acres of garden out by the high school and got around town on foot or by bicycle. Seeing this octogenarian crowd so busy, Curtis and Anne chastised each other whenever one complained about the aches and pains of aging.

When he came in with the fish and chicken, the conversation about challenges of the future was still ongoing. As he helped bring the dishes to the table, Cathy nudged him and whispered, "I need to tell you something—after dinner."

After a blessing Vickie, continued the talk about crowding in the town and in their own homes, "Now, the rooms are big in this house, of course, but your furniture leaves space and not every piece of wall has a painting or a clock or some sort of hanging on it."

Mark laughed. "It's easier when you're moving; you can weed as you go." To himself he admitted that he liked to have his things around him. They created a stability and a security that were important. Cathy was much more comfortable with flux.

"We all have the baggage of long lives in our houses," admitted Carl. "Our own things plus more given to us by children. And we can't part with it. It's just who we are, but sometimes I feel like a prisoner of my treasures."

Klara agreed. "Oh, my, but there's something in every corner. We've got footstools, coffee tables, floor lamps, end tables , sideboards, wine stands. We're positively hemmed in."

"Well," said Cathy, "let's enjoy where we are, then. Please find a place at the table, leaving me at this end so I can get up and down."

Only later, when their guests were stepped out on the deck to watch the moon rise over the river, did Mark find out what was discussed while he was working outside with the grill.

She looked out to be sure the others wouldn't be able to hear. "I learned some things at Darlene's, and I just realized how all the talk about 'broiler factories' the other day might have affected the men. Carl was among the soldiers who 'liberated' Buchenwald. The talk of chicken carcasses piled up have reminded him of what he'd seen."

Mark paused with a dish in his hand. Pictures he'd seen in history classes years ago came to mind. As did the phrase from somewhere: "corpses stacked like corded firewood." He concluded, "Still, that was a long time ago. And we're talking about chickens."

"Maybe. But Patrick, too, he saw things in Burma . . . the Thailand-Burma Railway, which some call the Death Railway. The Japanese used forced labor--Dutch, Australian, and others--to build it. Nobody knows how many died in their labor camps."

Mark frowned. "My own war spawned massacres, too. The Killing Fields in Cambodia were a consequence of the

US war. But I was not an eyewitness."

"Vickie says the men never talk about it, except to each other. I wish there was a place for you all, somewhere free with enough room for whatever needed to come out to come out."

"You mean a man's Darlene's. Shhh, here come the ladies."

Mark turned quickly and asked Klara, Vickie, and Anne-Harriet, "Getting cool out there now?"

"Yes, but invigorating. Cathy, let us help with the cleaning up."

Cathy insisted, "Mark will finish. Come give me some advice on how to arrange photos on the mantel in the living room. There's space for every picture to stand out." As they turned toward the hall, she nodded him in the direction of the deck and mouthed, "Get out there with them."

He found that Carl and Patrick had wandered down across the yard and stepped out on his small dock. He joined them as, hands clasped behind their backs and rocking on their heels, they were reminiscing about wartime experience.

"As I recall," Carl was telling Patrick, "Your radios went out one time. Was it in Pyawbwe?"

"Somewhere close. About that same time, you know, you were cut off on the way to Ohrdrfu."

They gazed at the moon in silence, huge but shrinking slowly as it rose through thin clouds. "Rain tomorrow, looks to me," observed Patrick.

"The cotton can use it." Another pause. He turned to Mark. "Want to go with us and take a look at some fields tomorrow?

Nobody out there except us old-timers. But we can tell you a story or two."

Mark said to them, "I'd like that." To himself he thought: "There's more reason than I realized to host this July 4 celebration." To Cathy (later) he confessed: "I think I'm in."

Chapter Eleven: Stores.

After touring Patrick's farm and sharing stories with his senior senior neighbors, Mark began to view Staffordshire differently. Houses and stores were not just structures but historical markers. For instance, Vernon's Hardware Store on Main Street, run by another member of the Greatest Generation, was stocked with memories as well as goods.

Vernon Benson, the long-time proprietor, was famous for his booming voice and for keeping stock that has been succeeded by improved versions. You wouldn't find the latest pliers that convert to a pipe wrench, the impact-rated screwdriver designed to integrate hand and power tools. A titanium trim hammer with a replaceable steel face and grip was not to be seen. But if you hoped to replace an ancient screw-in fuse (rather than install circuit breakers) in your 100-year-old garage, Vernon had it—somewhere.

That didn't mean Mark wouldn't encounter a modern version of a traditional standard inside this store. Hoping, for instance, to find a grounded extension cord several days after he and Cathy had hosted their neighbors, Mark rounded a row of shelves and almost bumped into a woman of the present. He stepped back to give her room, but almost fell back as she said with mild disgust, "You'd think a store like this would have a grass whip, wouldn't you?"

Mark had seen no one who looked like this in Staffordshire. Slim, with the kind of fitness regular gym visits produced, classic high cheekbones, dark hair pulled back under a headband, she would fit in with guests at an upscale urban hotel.

"Oh, um, yes," he admitted. "Whatever Vernon stocked back in the '50s is here, but little has been added to shelves since. The store's almost an antique itself. You're new in town?"

She put out a hand and tilted her head back to look him intently in the eyes. "Yes, Caroline Lee." She pronounced it Ca-ro-*lyne*, with emphasis on the last syllable. Mark tried not to look where the top two buttons of her blouse were unfastened She explained, "My husband Randy and I bought the little store—well, once a store—on Main Street." She gestured south. He'd seen the for-sale sign and knew the building.

"Ah. Mark Nelson, on Water Street." He gestured east. "There's an Ace Hardware out by the Food Lion. And Walmart is in Harbor City."

Caro-lyne winked and squeezed his arm. "I must get you to take me to one of those places."

He watched her walk away—with interest.

"See something you like?" asked Cathy, who'd been to the drug store at the other end of the block and come up behind him. "In Vernon's, of course."

"Oh, uh, no. Just . . ."

"Um-hm," she said. "I guess I'd better get you home before you . . . lose your way."

On their way, they passed the house of Charlene Brown,

the retired Marine and now their on Water Street. She was weeding a bed of flowers in her side yard. Pulling off her gloves, she waved to chairs on her porch. "Come sit. Bring me up to date about the 4th."

"We're still debating the project, but with a more positive view," Mark admitted, holding the back of one chair for Cathy. "It's not that it's so much work, is understanding the complex social dynamics of a Southern small town."

Charlene chuckled. "And now traditional racial lines are a bit blurred, aren't they? Well, even our regional identity is less clear. Have you met the Lees, the couple that bought the little store—well, once a store—on Main Street?"

Cathy grinned, cocking her head at Mak. "He just met her."

Charlene smiled and waited to see if either would say more, then explained, "Big city, East Coast. They looked at property at the Colony but ended up in that narrow two-story frame building. I guess they'll fix it up, but it probably means they're not really going to live here."

"A vacation home, but not on the water. That is odd. But how do you know all this?"

"As someone in real estate, I have my contacts. The Lees have been asking a lot of questions about town governance and policies. I feel like they're up to more than having a weekend getaway 600 miles from home."

Cathy added, "I don't see a need for a real store there, though a permanent bakery would be a good addition to the itinerant Whole Donut van."

Charlene sighed. "Agreed. I'll admit that I wonder about their motives. They're obviously well off, and I would say belong in a more upscale, um. . . stylish community. Why buy an old shop with no future in an out-of-the-way little town?"

The three neighbors left the topic there, and the Nelsons continued home. In part to direct conversation away from Ca-ro-*lyne* Lee and his reaction to her, Mark asked if he'd ever told her about his boyhood scheme to create a neighborhood store just for kids.

"If I said you had, would that stop you from telling me again."

"Of course not. I was just reminded of it by the fact that an old store here is going to be brought back."

"I hope you're not proposing we start a neighborhood store in your second childhood?"

"Not a bit, though it would be an exercise of American free enterprise. I wonder what products the Lees plan to stock and what clientele they hope to find in a town of 2,000 in a rural county."

"Good point. We've got drug store, hardware, grocery, bank. Sal's Junk Shop, down on West Street, sells all sorts of stuff on consignment. Whatever someone can't find in else-where, they'll probably find in there—in time."

Mark had stopped in Sal's several times to browse and was struck by the odd collection of kitchen appliances, garden tools, and outdoor furniture. It would be, as James Baldwin had ad-vised, a place to go if they needed things for the 4th; but it was so cluttered that specific items would be hard to locate.

"So," he asked, "what did you see in the drug store?"

She grinned, "As a matter of fact, I saw Randy Lee, hus-band of the woman in the tight pants you were watching by Vernon's."

"Ah, was he as . . . as fit as his wife?"

"I believe he was, and is. He wore pants that showed off his charms. You won't guess how those two gorgeous individuals met?"

"Oh, you had a chat, then, with the hot new store owner yet you teased me about meeting his wife?"

"I did. That's what I'm confessing I learned that he ran a blackjack table in Atlantic City. She, a recent divorcee, was on an extravagant weekend funded by a settlement very much in her favor."

They reached their front porch, and Mark unlocked the door. The regular folks on Anne-Harriet's porch said there was no need to lock doors in Staffordshire; but this was a life-long habit Mark found hard to abandon.

Sitting on a stool at the kitchen counter, he resumed their talk of the Lees. "I'm guessing Caro-lyne *lost* thousands in Atlantic City. We know how the odds are stacked in the table's favor from the get-go. And an angry divorcee might enjoy throwing her ex's money away"

"In fact, she won thousands. And came back a month later and won again. Didn't seem to matter, Randy said, if she won or lost. Free and easy was her style."

"Interesting. We talk about gamblers as addicts, prisoners of the habit, but maybe she's an exception who can take it up and put it down. So, one night they got married in Vegas? Or can you do that in Atlantic City, too?"

"You can. There are agencies that will procure a license at 11:00 pm and play 'Here Comes the Bride' at midnight in their chapel. That's what the Lees did; and, apparently, it's going into the fifth year—with enough money to purchase and renovate a second home."

Mark noted, "You had a pretty long talk with someone you just bumped into at the drug store."

"Well, we're still sort of new in town ourselves, so I was just making him feel welcome by listening to his story. I think he's still dazzled by his good fortune. He went from a lowly wage earner to being independently wealthy in less than month."

"That is rare, an American rags-to-riches story but not by the Horatio Alger method. This is a different scenario, but do you remember watching *The Americans*? People weren't what they seemed. The central characters. Elizabeth and Phillip Jennings, the couple living in suburban DC, were, in fact, Russian spies embedded during the Cold War."

"I remember you practically drooled at Keri Russell's love scenes?"

"Well," he responded, "you didn't look away when Matthew Rhys seduced his share of women."

The television Jennings were a sexy couple, occasionally seducing each other, but mostly using their charms to get secrets from American officials whose mouths would fall open in desire and spill vital government information.

"So, you're thinking this mysterious couple, the Lees from the Northeast, are really spies embedding themselves in Staffordshire to sabotage our Independence Day party?"

Mark clucked his tongue. "As you remember, John Smith alerted us to the possibility of a Russian invasion where and when we least expect it."

Then he asked himself what would be discovered if the

surface identities of Staffordshire residents turned out to be illusions like the Jennings family blending into the suburban Virginia scene. What would happen if masks were dropped, and the truth laid bare?

There were oddities Mark and Cathy had already puzzled over. What was Charlene's Marine past? Was The Whole Donut van a traveling CIA eavesdropping operation, monitoring the whole East Coast? Why was Beverly the lawyer doing manual labor in a town where some Sandy Point (CIA, DOD, Homeland Security?) personnel lived? Was Raymond Winston as out of it as he seemed, or was he using his reputation as a disguise to keep track of townspeople?

Would a celebration of Independence Day, if it even happened, mean anything except that we're all free to be whatever we want to be in public and in secret? Most scary of all, what if a spirit of freedom inspired Cathy to insist she needed that "space" truly unhappy spouses demand when a marriage is coming apart.

He concluded that he should come up with a way to celebrate their wedding anniversary that would convince her of his devotion. But what would that be and how could he make it happen on the day after the increasingly formidable July 4 event?

Chapter Twelve: Boom

"Patrick has invited me to go out on his boat tomorrow, the Liberty," reported Mark later in the week. "It might take up much of at the day."

"That's fine," said Cathy. "I have my hair appointment at Darlene's. I may need half a day to recover from indoctrination."

"I wouldn't be surprised. But it is a chance to learn what's being said in town about the upcoming holiday. See if anyone knows more about the Lees, the newcomers."

"Only if you find out more about the old-timers."

"Agreed."

In fact, Mark wished his 90-year-old neighbor would educate him beyond local history. Patrick was a model, he felt, for aging gracefully.

He and his wife Vickie were active in their late 80s, regularly attending both church and Sunday school. He was an on-again, off-again officer in the Rotary, and she played bridge with two different groups. They were up to date on local and national events.

Their views on race had evolved with the New South's. Patrick had grown up on a farm west of town and knew the physical costs of labor experienced by the less educated children in the county. After he graduated from college and joined the military at the start of World War II, he realized how much better his education had been than the schooling of black children he'd played with on the farm.

One of his retirement passions was sailing *Liberty*, a 22-foot Hereshoff Eagle. The boat was distinguished from the more conventional local boats by its gaff rigging. The jib and an oversized main sail would pull it over on its side in strong winds to the point that the crew were almost standing vertically, their feet on one bench and their hips back against the other. But it had sandbag ballast in the hull, and with an expert skipper at the helm, was in no danger of capsizing.

Everyone living downriver was used to the sight of the green hull, its white sails with broad red horizontal bars full in the wind. He and whoever else might be on board would wave to the scattered house, knowing most of the residents. The boat's passing was taken as a sign that all was well in the Staffordshire community. Mark also saw it as a confirmation of underwater surveillance man, John Smith's philosophy—an embodiment of escape from the confinements of the everyday.

Mark had first seen Liberty under sail on a blustery summer day several years earlier. Patrick's two granddaughters, in their early twenties, were helping control the heeling by standing on the starboard rail, holding lines tied high to the mast and leaning out over the water. It was so inspiring a vision that Mark determined to be included on future voyages no matter how inexperienced he was. And he claimed he'd build his own wooden boat one day.

A lot of the shoreline he and Patrick would see today was farmland or cypress swamp. Handy woman/lawyer Beverly Foster had grown up somewhere on the south shore, and she and Patrick probably knew about things that had happened over the years in these remote places. Mark hoped for an opportunity to ask Patrick about the illicit liquor trade during the Depression Beverly had mentioned.

He'd never told Cathy how many empty pint bottles of cheap whiskey he'd found in the garage when they first moved in, left there, he assumed, by a Winston. He surmised that that individual liked having his private supply out of public sight. Mark dropped a few bottles at a time into their weekly recycling, not wanting to create the impression that he was the heavy drinker.

A they set out for the day's journey, Patrick observed, "I understand you're meeting more of the locals," He was using the outboard motor to pull away from the mooring.

"It's more they're introducing themselves to me. There's

Beverly, who, thanks to Cathy, now is my employee."

"She's a good sort. And I understand Thomas Beard is claiming you've contracted him for fireworks as usual."

"Interesting. I did meet him standing in line at the Whole Donut Van. And he acted as if this was a done deal, but I was careful not to confirm it."

"Take the tiller for a bit, while I haul up and tie off the sails. Steady as you go."

Although the wind was mild at this time in the morning, Mark was still nervous at the helm. "You know," he confessed, "I'm less keen on fireworks than a lot of folks."

Patrick nodded. "Veterans can be that way. We've heard enough noise in our lifetimes."

"I don't have flashbacks, but I have come to question the need for it all. I suppose if he does it over the river and a good distance from where we are, I could put up with it."

Patrick shaded his eyes against the sun. "We might get as far as White Rock today. We've got a steady northeast wind." He looked up. "And there goes Dusty Sherman."

Mark saw a bright orange single-engine bi-plane over the north shore. It dipped down suddenly, flew low over fields, and left behind clouds of white dust. "He's really low. What's he doing?"

"Spraying chemicals on the new crops now that the winter wheat is in. Dusty, Jr. and his dad, the first Dusty, have been doing it for thirty years. Both Air Force vets, good fliers."

"Ah," said Mark, making a mental note not to tell Cathy about what was likely environmentally harmful.

He had heard about the small community of homes they might reach today. White Rock was unincorporated, not much more than a neighborhood of perhaps twenty homes scattered around the opening of Wilson's Creek. Some residents chose to stay in places like it to avoid the encroachment of newcomers. It was closer to Sandy Point though, so the sound of testing explosives was greater than it was in town.

"You'd be showing me something new with White Rock," Mark told Patrick.

"Something old, too. This whole area was settled from the coast inland in the 17th century, with later generations moving away from rough weather and . . . and, well, pirates."

"I've read about Blackbeard, of course. I thought he and his like stayed closer to the sea, but is it believed some came this far, making White Rock a hideaway from the big ships?"

"No, it would be too shallow in these waters. But if you take the word of some old-timers, Blackbeard fathered a number of children and some of his descendants are among current residents of White Rock."

"That may be the same as everyone in Virginia being descendant of Pocahontas."

"Pull the jib in a bit there," said Patrick, gesturing to the starboard cleat.

"Aye, aye." (He couldn't resist saying it."

"The only one you might worry about is Beard. When I was growing up and sailing with my friends, Thomas' father was someone to be avoided. He put crab pots out without markers, and, if you were close to one of his fields, he would fire a shotgun over the water as a warning to stay away."

"But no markers, that makes it tough."

"His sister, the current Thomas' aunt, was even more to be feared. In fact, now that I think about it, she might be a descendant of a pirate. She was pretty much ungovernable."

"The term would fit pirates, I suppose—free spirits on the open seas. They respected no laws, no countries, no one unless they had greater firepower."

"She was that way. A frequent truant from school, she would shoplift, make off with other students' school supplies, take things from people's porches. She'd sell it all to buy drink. Not legally, of course; but moonshine was easy to come by even after Prohibition ended."

"Beverly hinted there might still be stills in these woods."

"I couldn't comment on that. I will say this, though: the booze Thoms' aunt bought enabled her to recruit others for clandestine raids around town. I wouldn't call what came to be 'a gang,' but Sally could organize some pretty rowdy parties. There were places along the river where, on a clear night, you could see smoke rising and light flickering."

"Teenage fun? Or a witches' Satanic rite?"

Patrick asked, "How would I know?" But Mark thought the lifting of his eyebrows and something close to a wink suggested he might indeed know. And that was when he began to suspect Patrick had invited him along today not just to assist with the boat.

He asked, "She's no longer with us, right? The female descendant of pirates who roamed wild along the river decades ago?"

"Yes, she's gone, but there are adventurous sorts around

here who have similar views what we think is proper behavior. Pulling off a neighborhood block party without unpleasant confrontations will be quite a feat."

A feat? thought Mark. He'd prefer Patrick had said, a challenge or a sign of underlying harmony. Was he anticipating something specific that would undo the celebration? Pirates?

Patrick looked east again into the sun and said, "Let's get ready to come about. We'll have to leave White Rock for another day."

"Ready to come about, Captain," said Mark.

He'd told Cathy about the danger of being knocked out by the swinging boom, and she'd been genuinely alarmed. He concluded that she wanted him to stay alive at least long enough to host the July 4 celebration, but to plan a July 6 wedding anniversary? He still had no clear idea what outing he should propose to show his appreciation.

Chapter Thirteen: Caves

"So," began Cathy, "food and dress."

"Pardon?" She and Mark were in the kitchen/family room area preparing dinner. Mark was idly thinking about the descendants of pirates invading the July 4 party.

"At Darlene's," Cathy went on, "I learned we need to review dress and food choices, putting the right suggestions on our invitation."

"Ah Yes, if we go ahead, that is. 'Party casual' for both seems simple enough to me."

Their meal was simple: she was opening a container of frozen homemade bean soup and he would open a tube of Pillsbury frozen crescent rolls.

"You innocent man! I've learned that lots of our neighbors feel patriotism must show through what we wear, what we cook, what we say, the songs we sing. Apparently, we should be prepared for—and perhaps encourage—red, white, and blue striped ties, Mount Rushmore T-shirts, Uncle Sam hats, cell phones playing "The Star-Spangled Banner" and "America the Beautiful.""

An image of what the Simpson's granddaughter might wear took shape in Mark's brain. Low slung jeans revealing a small American flag tattoo in the small of her back, untucked stars and stripes blouse with the tails tied across her bare belly.

"The same goes for prepared dishes, I suppose," he said. "I hope serving hamburgers and hot dogs is American enough, but I guess we should consider cups, paper plates, and napkins in red, white, and blue. Oh, and apple pie."

Cathy squeezed the soup from its plastic container into a pot with a little water to begin warming. Mark rapped the crescent roll tube on the counter, and the dough bulged out of the opening like a horde of children bursting from a school building at the end of a day.

Rather than folding individual triangles into crescents, Mark liked to stretch the whole tube lengthwise and slice the resulting longer roll. That made what was called "wheat stalk bread." He slid it into the refrigerator. When the soup was fully thawed, he'd bake the bread for ten minutes.

Cathy frowned. "I'm trusting there will be no Confederate flags."

"I hope so, too" said Mark. "But colonial garb is possible.

Hmm, I wonder if we'll have to ask everyone to check guns at the door. I don't even know the laws in this state. Is concealed carry legal?"

"I think worrying about such things will distort our notion of what this is all about. You'd be looking at anyone wearing a Betsy Ross dress for the derringer strapped to the thigh and me for daggers tucked into General Grant pants."

"Well," insisted Mark, "I do fear the political climate these days contains a potential for violence in small towns as well as big cities."

They stepped around the counter that separated the kitchen from the family room. They would keep the soup on warm while she reviewed the news on her iPad and he studied the financial page in an online newspaper.

As she sat on the sofa, Cathy said, "Now here's something potentially interesting in the area's past that might affect the present: *Slave Escapes & the Underground Railroad in North Carolina.* I was inspired to buy it after seeing the plaque in Edenton Harbor City about Harriet Jacobs."

"Right. She escaped slavery after hiding . . . how many years was it?"

"Seven. In an attic so low she couldn't stand up straight. She took refuge there to escape her owner who insisted on having sex with her. It was so dark in her tiny hiding place she could barely read or sew."

Mark said, "She became an advocate for change, a patriot in a true sense."

"It's interesting what she read, too: the *Bible* for strength and newspapers to learn about life outside slavery. Remember, she could sometimes observe her own children through a crack in the attic wall, but never speak with them—it would endanger them all."

"We're living in times of change," noted Mark. "Stories like hers are being recovered and read more widely—brought out of hiding, you might say, as she was. I hear 'Lift Every Voice and Sing' now and then, which I never did growing up."

"You know, I almost wanted to bring Harriet Jacobs up in our neighbor Anne-Harriet's story about 'walking the chickens.' We kept agreeing that the way the birds were crowded together in 'broiler factories' was terrible, and I could have gone from there to that attic in Edenton."

Mark sighed. "We will have to be careful not to make what we think are innocent comments on Independence Day. Some could irritate a neighbor angry about revisionist history."

Cathy concluded. "Well, the first amendment is another thing we need to be ready for, assuming we are hosts. Speech is open in our democracy, but you're right that we should stay away from comments that might be triggers."

"In that vein, let me take a look at your book."

She declared it was time to put in the bread in, so his review of The Underground Railway had to wait until after dinner. When he did begin reading late, Mark found it an intriguing account, opening up areas of local history that he'd not known.

He and Cathy had driven by the Dismal Swamp on trips up to Norfolk, but never stopped to read historical markers that explained how it was a major destination for escaped slaves. He had simply been amused to see signs about bears crossing highways—ursine right of way?

Blacks before the Civil War knew the Swamp well, as their

ancestors had been made to dig a canal there by hand in the early 19th century. Snakes, insects, bears, and bobcats made it a dangerous environment; and no one wanted to pursue desperate people in there.

From the Swamp, enslaved people could travel to Harbor City and then by boat to freedom, working as stewards and cooks to earn their passage. Harriet Jacobs made her escape by water, but, like all the others, was always in danger of capture and being returned to slavery.

Mark thought of the space above their own garage. Yes, it was built after slavery was abolished, but what if, he wondered, a hiding place had been needed during the Jim Crow years for falsely accused or suspected people? He learned from a web museum of black history based in Ash Grove, Missouri, that a Jim Crow mentality had shaped the culture where he'd grown up.

In the early twentieth century the Ozark region around Springfield saw so much violence against blacks, including lynching, that many fled to safer regions of the country and never returned.

A few hundred miles west is Tulsa, Oklahoma, where a coordinated attack occurred on what was known as "Black Wall Street," thirty-five square blocks of black owned homes and businesses, left 800 residents injured and thousands interned.

Missouri is generally classified as part of the Midwest, but attitudes in the southern third are similar to those in bordering Kentucky, Tennessee, and Arkansas. And Missouri had been a slave state (a fact had been gently obscured in his high school classes). Mark hadn't wondered if there were hideouts for escaping slaves along underground railway routes. Missouri's limestone geology includes many caves. Maybe they'd later provided refuge.

Mark's youthful experiences of caves involved a school

tour of Meramec Caverns and a family visit to Onondaga Caverns. Each of these geological wonders is large enough to ride a horse in, and legend says Jesse James used Meramec as a hideout for his whole gang. Few people on the standard tours felt trapped inside.

It was in a cave closer to home that Mark had his first experience of alcohol; and rather than feeling confinement in that tight space, he had felt liberated.

His family was neither religious nor overly strict, but his parents drank rarely. And in high school, he didn't hang out with kids who knew how to get around the twenty-one-year-old legal age limit for buying liquor. Unspoken social rules did as much as official policy to restrain him and his friends in those years. The next decades, however, unlocked inhibitions society didn't realize it had been holding in check .

Over the weekend of Mark's class graduation, one of his friends heard from one of his friends (a widening circle of different cliques) that there was to be an informal party in a cave on a farm owned by some other classmate's grandparents.

You could stand in the front part of the cave, where a campfire produced enough light to reveal the dark outlines of classmates. But deeper in the hillside was a tunnel that led to a tin tub full of ice and beer. The minute Mark arrived someone stepped out of the shadows and put a cold can in his hand.

"This'll wake up the sleeping genie in your head," said a girl, her identity hidden in the dark. Another hand, perhaps belonging to another girl, produced an opener. Not wanting to reveal that he was a novice at this sort of thing, Mark tipped the can back, swallowed a series of mouthfuls, smiled, and belched.

As the night went on, and successive cans appeared in his hands, a new landscape of freedom opened up in his vision of the future after high school. Being drafted into the military and serving in Vietnam, however, prevented his becoming a "child of the 60's."

Chapter Fourteen: Hammers

"There is one thing I forgot to tell you that may affect your attitude about July 4," Cathy told him later in the week as they were playing Scrabble on the screen porch. "About fireworks."

"Okay. Shoot, so to speak."

"Well, the ladies were talking at Darlene's about the Colony's fireworks. It's a big, big deal out there."

"That's fine with me. It's seven miles down the river, so flashes and booms will be nicely distanced."

"Yes, but some in town want to make a big response. Sort of bang and blaze back."

"Hmm. Let me think about this. I don't want to turn Thomas Beard loose. Given the burn marks on his body, he might somehow set the river on fire."

Cathy said, "Perhaps we can set a standard of moderation rather than rivalry."

Mark rubbed his chin. "We might use town regulations to justify a modest display. I should look into the rules for getting a permit."

"No permit needed," said someone coming down the driveway. Mark jumped.

He and Cathy then saw Raymond Winston, their garage guest, come around the azalea bushes bordering the porch and follow the short sidewalk to the steps.

"Oh?" asked Cathy, smiling.

"Fireworks Tom has a standing permit, having done this . . . well, forever," explained Ray, opening the screen door and pulling a chair up to the little table where the Scrabble game was placed. "Who's winning today?"

"Too early to tell," said Mark, turning his rack of letters away so their guest couldn't see them and tell Cathy the letters he was seeing. She got up and said, "Coffee? We're ready for our second cup of the morning."

"Why, that would be most kind, ma'am. You all are natural hosts. And I'll return your kindness with some advice."

Mark rolled his eyes, wondering what brought this man back to the Winston House. His cousin, Officer James Winston, had said he was out at a family farm. He was also dressed more carefully today. Instead of camouflage pants and an old Army fatigue jacket, he was wearing Dickie work clothes.

"You see, my friend," Ray explained to Mark. "You're not going to change customs around here easily. You need to relax and fit it; then, over time, you can make, um, gentle suggestions about how things are done. Let me tell you about my Uncle Julius."

Cathy set the coffee thermos, cream, and sugar on the table, handing Ray a cup. "Please help yourself. Julius is another family member here in Persimmon County?"

"He was a blacksmith, ma'am, shoeing horses and repairing machinery at a shop down by the mill. You can still see the building he put up there after he came home from the war."

Another member of the Greatest Generation, thought Mark, sometimes called builders because they created new businesses when they came home and spurred prosperity for the country. He was pretty sure the building was lost when the family tobacco mill burned. Ray was mixing memories of the past with his sense of the present, although he seemed more sober and focused than when he had brandished a pitchfork at Mark in his garage.

Cathy said, "I would have thought that trade was dying out about that time."

"True, enough," Raymond admitted, "but more slowly here than in other places. My uncle made do by repairing metal gates, wheelbarrows, farm machine parts. He didn't want to work for 'The Man,' so he gambled everything on his beer can bicycle."

"I'm afraid to ask," admitted Mark. "But what would a beer can bicycle be?"

"Well, you know how kids look for cans thrown into roadside ditches or alleys, turn them in for pennies?"

Cathy nodded, "Of course. Even I did that to get my favorite Chupa Chups."

He grinned. "Uncle Julius would buy them up and use them to build bicycles modeled on the Chinese Flying Pigeon, which he'd learned about in Burma during the war. He thought he could beat out Western Auto that sold Schwinn's, but people had become used to buying such things through Sears Roebuck and Montgomery Ward. Their catalogs opened up a world of goods to small towns like this, you know."

Mark did, having battled with his siblings to have his turn turning the pages of a new issue. He and his older brother wanted to inspect images in the women's wear section. Their younger sister, he learned much later, had her interests as well. "So, what did he do?"

"Accepted the way things are . . . pretty much."

Cathy raised her eyebrows. "There were exceptions?"

"Don't want to go into the details, ma'am; but he did find a few operations willing to let him modernize their equipment—off the books, you see, and off the main roads."

Mark thought about the "adventurous sorts" Patrick had said were still living downriver, likely moonshiners. That would mean Julious had gone off the grid like Raymond.

Cathy asked Ray, "How do you know all this about bicycle history? From Uncle Julius?"

Mark knew that bicycles had opened up the world for people who could not afford horses or cars, giving them a freedom of mobility overnight. Cathy knew women on bicycles represented a dramatic breaking of stereotypes—their own wheels!

Raymond smiled. "You know what they say: join the military and see the world. Chinese products, including bicycles were all over Vietnam. And I had . . . um, . . some time for reading over there. I even explored ancient Chinese literature."

"The *Art of War,* perhaps," offered Mark. "Sun Tzu 's masterpiece has been around for 2,500 years and is still considered a classic."

"Yeah. 'In the midst of chaos, there is also opportunity.' That . . . and their poetry," Ray smiled and then said more seriously, "There's an ancient Chinese poem I've come to like. 'Blue Smoke War; White Bones Men.' The terms would be shown as pictures in the original, of course, not letters. I found an English version; 'Blue is the smoke of war; white are the bones of men.'"

Cathy frowned. "I'm still not sure I understand it."

Ray smiled. "It's taken me a long time, but this is what I think. The blue smoke puts us away from the black smoke of explosion and destruction, aware of what's happening, but we're not in the middle of combustion. The white bones back us farther off in a time frame, as the battle was long ago and the costs have been fixed in the landscape."

"So," concluded Mark, "the poem is a statement of resignation? This is just the way things have always been and always will be?"

"Yes, but it's also about Innnn-DE-PEN-DENCE." He stretched out the first syllable and stressed the last three. "You know how we said it, brother: 'There it is.'"

Cathy concurred. "Throughout history, humans haven't been able to exist without war; but war ends human existence."

Mark added, "So, to survive, we have to put this paradox into a frame—like the six words in two balanced phrases—and learn to accept it, become resigned to it?" Then he frowned. "Another thing we used say is, 'sheee-it.'"

Ray clapped him on the back. "That we did, my friend. Now, be careful playing that 'U' you have among your Scrabble tiles; someone else might be holding a 'Q' to use with it."

When he'd gone—and Cathy had played 'quickly' for 94 points—Mark asked, "Is that scholar of classical philosophy the same guy who a few weeks ago thought I was the Winston family handyman?"

Cathy chuckled. "Just another side of the same man, I'd say. Today he's got his days and nights straight."

Chapter Fifteen: Stock

After Ray had gone on "to dispense wisdom to others," Cathy asked Mark, "Would you like to hear about Lees' plans for their store? They seem eager to get opinions about its potential."

"I'm not sure we're the best appraisers. New to the community, at least as full-time residents, and with no professional or even amateur experience in retail." He wondered to himself if Cathy was seeing this as some sort of test for him, encountering the woman who was likely confident of her effect on men.

Cathy explained, "I think she wants to get as many takes on it as she can, both in terms of design and potential stock. She told me that they were going to close in the front and side porches for goods and services, living in the rest of the house. And I liked her husband."

"That sounds like they will be here full time. I thought Charlene didn't see them in that way. More that they were here for some short-term project."

"Well, I'm curious . . . and I agreed to stop by this afternoon."

Mark didn't think it wise not to accompany her. She'd been appreciative of Randy's good looks. He also envisioned Caro-*lyne* in carpenter's dress, a tool belt hanging low over canvas cargo pants, and then banished it from his thoughts.

The idea of the store, though, made him recall his and Billy's doomed neighborhood kids' store. He and Billy's youthful entrepreneurial plans had been based on faulty childhood assumptions and an ignorance of the forces that drove the adult world.

A neighbor, whom they knew only as "Old Man Simpson," had let them use his old one-car garage as their store. They never knew he kept a stock of pornography in the slant-roofed room off the back of the building (off-limits to them). It was mild stuff by today's standards, but *Playboy* and its competition at the time were not readily attainable.

The kids' store survived briefly (before folding due to bankruptcy), but only as a cover for the coming and going of adult customers in the house out front. It was thought Simpson also hosted a friendly poker table on Thursday nights, another pastime in small-town America not pictured by Noman Rockwell on a cover of *The Saturday Evening Post*. The boys would learn that both operations were very profitable.

Discovering what a child's eyes are conditioned not to see in the 1950s should have make Mark look beneath the surface of the tour Caro-*lyne* gave him and Cathy in the 21st century. The eyes of an adult, though, can be blind in other ways.

At their store Randy referred all questions of appearance to Cathy—what colors to use, whether to refresh or sand and redo the floors, the best kinds of drapes, curtains, lighting. Mark noted that he was a handsome man, slender but fit like his wife. He was wearing faded blue jeans and a T-shirt with "RR" printed in a circle over the pocket. Mark saw that Cathy looked him over carefully.

Caro-*lyne* needed nothing, thought Mark, like the stylistic upgrades being planned for the building. She wore designer jeans and a linen top. She directed all her observations and questions about product display, advertising, and pricing to Mark.

"This will be our office," she said, pulling him into what had been a pantry off the kitchen and the side porch. He could see the sound system that was piping jazz tunes throughout the building. "We're not expecting to make it rich—um, a second time—but to provide something for the community, at least some of our fellow residents."

"Ah, not exactly non-profit," agreed Mark, "but not operating at a loss either. "I don't think you'll have a rival in boutique items."

He glanced back to the front of the store. Randy was leaning close to Cathy, talking intently, gesturing. Was he telling more of his past or suggesting how she could be part of his future?

Caro-lyne explained, "We'll keep a low inventory of most items: purses, shoes, dresses, hats. Some things . . . um . . . won't be displayed, though." She stepped close, tilted her head, and whispered in his ear. "They'll be for our select clientele."

"Ah." Mark breathed in her jasmine perfume, raised his eyebrows in curiosity. He heard Diana Krall crooning "Peel me a grape."

Caro-*lyne* straightened up. "You know, on another topic entirely, I've heard that drugs are not hard to find in Staffordshire, if you know where to ask."

"I . . . I actually don't know. But it's true, I think, that most small towns are on a supply chain. And I read somewhere that law enforcement spends little time looking into them; so smaller dealers operate pretty freely."

Mark had, in fact, heard that there was one street in town you could drive down, slow at an intersection where young men seemed to be loitering, and offers would come to you. But beer, wine, and liquor were the choice of seniors like him.

"Of course," Caro-lyne went on, "we're talking about pot mostly, when you don't have a college crowd. Perhaps meth, ecstasy, some crack. But, you know, there's a strong market in big cities for more upscale new drugs law enforcement doesn't even know to look out for. In the spirit of free enterprise, we could have a market for them, especially among the residents at the Colony."

She leaned a little closer, and Mark felt her shoulder touch his. He remembered the demand for fireworks on the Fourth of July. He saw flashes and heard booms.

Looking for escape, he glanced through the pantry door to where Cathy was nodding at Randy. He caught her eye, and she made a simple but unequivocal gesture, one she and many a mother has made over generations. (Some fathers, too, but he associated this with women.)

He and Cathy had seen this means of communication at a restaurant where they'd had lunch a week or so earlier, a down-home country place popular with families. A mother two tables over from their booth took her three children to the restrooms. Mark was casually watching. When the mother and children went behind a screen that shielded the doors to Men's and Ladies', though, he couldn't tell everything that was happening. He had thought it was the boy who needed to go (or was just curious); and he was young enough that the mother would want to stay close.

As the boy went into the Men's, one sister went into the Ladies'; but the other girl, the older one, slipped away and headed for the gum ball machine. Although Mark couldn't see

Mom completely (half of her body was behind the screen), she must have sensed the escape. In a way some parents can command their children's attention without saying a word, she made her daughter stop, turn around, and look at her.

One of the mother's arms extended straight down her side, and a single straight finger pointed to a spot on the floor beside her. The gesture meant: "Here. Now!"

From the front of the Lees' store, Cathy made exactly the same gesture to Mark. He did what the daughter did.

When they were back in their house, Cathy said, "I need to make a confession."

"Oh?" Mark welcomed this, fearful that she was going to ask why he had been so close to Caro-*lyne* and what sweet somethings she was whispering in his ear. He pulled a beer from the refrigerator and a bottle of Chardonnay for her.

Cathy said, "I learned that Randy was not just a blackjack dealer. He's had . . . other careers."

"Please tell." He poured her a glass of wine and opened the beer for himself.

"First, let me explain that he grew up poor somewhere in the Midwest, maybe Arkansas. His parents were working class and couldn't afford for him to go to college, so he tried construction, landscaping, even—after his parents died--circus work."

Marked nodded. "He did have obstacles on the path to prosperity. In the circus, what was he? Lion tamer, acrobat, knife thrower? I hope he didn't have Caro-lyne stand up against the wall and outline her . . . her figure with knives."

"No. He was behind the scenes, putting up and taking

down tents, platforms, booths. It was hard work, and he was always on the road."

"It was a nice road that led to Atlantic City, it seems. It does remind me, though, of how much a college education means, or at least has meant. Your nursing degree and mine in marketing gave us opportunities to move in many directions. We weren't limited by booms or busts the way so many are. We'll always need medicine, and someone has to tell the story."

She sipped her wine. "I really think, though, that Randy's a nice man. Unpretentious, down to earth, grateful for what's come his way."

Mark admitted, "I'm a little less sure about her character. I'm like Charlene, wondering what she plans for this little store. She . . . gave me some hints."

Cathy didn't seem to want to know about that. "In Atlantic City, Randy was a dancer as well as blackjack dealer."

"Ah. In those extravaganza shows—chorus lines and special effects and pyrotechnics."

"His was a more . . . restricted venue."

"Oh?"

"In fact, he was a male dancer, small club, select audience."

"I guess you mean a stripper." Mark laughed, imagining women stuffing money in his G-string as he looked down over his shoulder from the stage. "Let me guess. I bet he performed as 'Randy Randy'! Do you think he could be persuaded to dance as Uncle Sam at our party?"

He said it as a joke, but he knew he had become more serious about the need to celebrate the national holiday . . . and to do it well. A clue about how he might do so would come, unexpectedly from his parents' generation.

But there was still the nagging question of what he should arrange to recognize his marriage's strength. Exotic dancing?

Chapter Sixteen: Signs

Because tradition held that every house on Water Street and on Main Street between the bridge and the Episcopal cemetery (five blocks in all) received a printed invitation to the July 4 celebration, Cathy and Mark decided to do a count to predict turnout. Each was also processing their provocative tour of the Lee house/store.

Of course, they knew some houses had absentee owners, and others had not been occupied for years and could be excluded from the survey. But the average number of guests for each house had to take into account out-of-town family members who usually attended.

"Let's take this map to identify homes," suggested Cathy, holding up the copy they'd picked up from the Chamber of Commerce. "Then we consult Beverly about likely guests."

"Okay," agreed Mark. "But you work that out, and I'll compose the invitation."

He didn't exactly resent the friendship the two women were establishing, but he continued to be irritated when Cathy asked Beverly to do things he felt he was perfectly capable of handling. The latest instance was building a set of stairs in the garage to access the loft.

"Can we have a slogan or catch phrase to include on our

invitation?" Mark asked, "Something like 'Bring Fourth.' You know, recalling Lincoln's Gettysburg Address, 'Brought forth on this continent . . .'"

"With emojis of fireworks being saluted by children with missing fingers, eye patches, bald patches on their heads?"

"Hummph. I just think it might be nice to spice up the invitation a bit, the same way your 'come hither' tattoo did the other night." Somewhere she'd found a temporary tattoo with the finger-curled design.

"Anne-Harriet loaned me copies from the past events," Cathy said. "You need to be consistent—what to bring, what's provided, etc. etc."

Mark saw the value of clarity, but he also wanted to make the design attractive. His career in public relations had made him realize images had become more successful in advertising than words as print culture faded with the advance of television and digital media.

Thinking about the graphics made him look more closely at signs he was seeing in front yards and at flags on porches. The latter seemed to be a new feature of homeownership: some houses sported university logos (especially U. of North Carolina or NC State); others included seasonal images (harvest symbols, snowflakes, spring growth, summer sport); and still more revealed the hobbies or passions of the owners— sailboats, flowers, fishing gear, golf clubs or tennis rackets. There were also signs warning that home security systems were in use.

Mark noted that certain homes had neatly lettered and colored signs on beautifully kept yards that identified the landscape services responsible for the display. The elegantly placed and pruned bushes, the weedless lawns of St. Augustine grass (that spread by its roots to snuff out competitors), and the ornamental fences surrounding flowerpots with bird-baths and cherub statuary seemed to have been dictated by an unspoken social consciousness.

"Are we seeing a proliferation of those," Mark asked, pointing to a sign reading,

"Scoop your Poop."

"Ha! Another thing I learned at Darlene's. There is a leash law and an 'understanding' that you dispose of your pet's droppings, but it seems not everyone takes that seriously. My favorite is 'Don't let your Dog / Water our Plants.'"

"Now, there's a different one," Cathy pointed. "Black Lives Matter."

"Yes. Interesting contrast, to be sure. You know, it reminds me of Mr. Jenson, my boss at the print shop where I worked as a teenager. He had signs that predated the environmental consciousness of today like, 'If Not Needed, Off Please.' There was one hanging at the bottom of the string you pulled to turn on the light in the storeroom. I liked the appeal to economy: use only what's necessary. And I liked the application of his business—sign making—to his own affairs."

He chuckled, "I think Mr. Jensen must have shared a similar background with my father. They were about the same age, and Dad taught his children frugality. If you lingered in the front doorway of our Sears-house (built to a cookie-cutter blueprint from precut materials shipped to the location), you would hear him say sharply, "Come in or go out." That is, don't let out the heat."

"Children of the Depression, our parents' generation could never abandon the restrictions they had as children. My dad has similar instructions, though they weren't printed out: "Clean your Plate. The children in China don't have such meals." Living within your means was his idea of living a just life. I fear we've lost track of that goal in this age of prosperity."

"Too true. Most of our friends, like us, live in houses twice as large as the ones they grew up in. I guess we rode an American post-Cold War boom into a new century. We're much less careful with our budgets than our parents were. We throw away leftovers, don't patch our clothes, buy new cars we don't really need."

He'd been happy to have that summer job at Jenson's through high school as it was a more reliable sources of income than his neighborhood store. After graduation he needed to save for his first year's tuition, but he hoped also to have enough spending money left over to pursue Veronica Hall, rising (and blooming) senior at Fairfield High. Inspired by his boss' signs, he thought the words, "All Dates / Require Contact," as he mapped out his campaign.

At work on the Heidelberg press he was assigned to run for small jobs, Mark had realized Mr. Jenson's signs could have been composed by his father: "All Boxes / Will be Flattened," "Closed Windows / Stop Drafts," and—perhaps Mark's favorite because of its poetic features—"Waste Water / Means Water Shortage." The injunctions came, Mark would learn, from the military, which regularly mounted efficiency campaigns.

Mark found out more about what was behind those signs when he was asked to use his new skills to make two signs that read in simple black letters, "ASK NOT." Mark thought it odd when Mr. Jenson put one in each of the windows that faced the street. Did he not want potential customers to inquire?

He "asked not" himself, though, so didn't understand what

was at play until the end of summer. In the meantime, he practiced college sweet talk, pixie dust to sprinkle on the lovely blond curls that lay around Veronica's sweet face.

Mark liked his work, running off advertising fliers and business brochures on the small off-set press. He also enjoyed the talk of his immediate superior, James (Jimmy) Hardcastle, who had tales (probably tall) to tell about life as a single young man. He'd stopped school at eleventh grade, gotten drafted, and spent one year stateside, two in Germany. He was one of the lucky ones who avoided the escalating conflict in Vietnam. "To Win a War / Don't go," he quoted someone. That one would come back to Mark after he was drafted.

Jimmy encouraged Mark's campaign to enjoy Veronica's company. "It's like printing a pamphlet," he explained. "You have to press your image on every page of her mind. Get her to think about you all day, then she'll be happy to see you that night."

Mark wasn't exactly clear how to do that. "Dream of Mark, / Dreamboat"?

It was easier to please Mr. Jenson: simply follow his injunctions: "Be on time, work steady, be proud of what you do." When Mr. Jenson rambled on about this or that, though, Mark had to make an extra effort to pretend interest.

One aspect of his boss' musing that consistently failed to catch Mark's interest: local and national events. He was, he asserted to himself, a worldly, rising college sophomore, not a small-town, high school boy. He was studying ideas of social organization in ancient civilizations and periods of European history, but the present was just a fuzzy backdrop for his daily life, the pursuit of delicious fantasy.

"There'll be a big July 4 parade this year," Mr. Jenson might announce one day. "You'll want to see it." Mark just looked forward to having an extra day off, not joining the crowd of old folks who would wave flags and cheer for liberty. Now, if he could get Veronica to watch with him from a secluded vantage point . . . .

"You're woolgathering," Cathy said punching him on the arm. "Are you paying any attention to houses, their likely residents, space for out-of-own guests. We're supposed to be planning for Bring Forth, remember."

He was pleased that she used the phrase.

"I'm considering layouts for the invitation," Mark said. "Eye-catching but not overdone, Southern sweet talk for . . . ."

Chapter Seventeen: Cargo

Mark was stopped in midstride and mid-sentence by the sight (eye-catching !) of a slender, bikini-clad young woman sunbathing in a chaise lounge in one of his neighbors' front yard. The house was owned by a married couple, both lawyers, who ran a real estate appraisal company and a bookstore in one downtown building. Hence their nickname, "the Bookstore Lawyers."

Cathy elbowed him in the ribs. "Eyes front, mister."

"That must be the Simpsons' granddaughter," he whispered, "the one who, we hear, will be doing tricks on the 4th."

"Already advertising?" questioned Cathy. "Couldn't she sunbathe down by the water?"

"Or beside the above-ground pool they have in back. This is . . . distracting."

Still thinking about yard signs on Water Street, Mark imagined a series of the old time Burma Shave-like signs on the sidewalk in front of the Simpsons': "Many men will drool, / babble and such. / But follow the old rule, / Look don't touch. / Close Shave."

At their house, they found Charlene Johnson sticking a flier inside the front porch storm door. She pulled it back and handed it to them. "Oh, hi, folks. I'm inviting you to attend the public meeting about the bridge project. Monday night, 7:00, the courthouse."

"Thanks," said Cathy. "Come in and let us hear your views over a cup of coffee."

At the table in their family room, they learned that their new neighbor was concerned about an effort by Main Street businesses to funnel traffic into that one block, ignoring the opportunity to broaden a positive impact in the larger community.

"Look at this," she said, spreading out a hand-drawn map of the town. "Notice Wharf Street, six blocks west of Main and parallel to it. The road goes out past the schools and connects to the bypass a few miles south of town,"

"I know the area where Wharf comes to a T with Main," said Mark. "There is a pretty much defunct strip mall there by the railroad tracks that backs up on the river."

"Exactly. The old shopping center and the surrounding area could be revitalized if the new bridge ended here." Charlene pointed to her map, where she'd penciled a bridge coming across from Rockwall to the northern edge of the old shopping center. "It could be a low bridge and wouldn't need a draw, as it's farther upriver."

"You're not thinking of condominiums going up along the

river there, are you?" asked Cathy. "I can see there is space."

"I'm thinking modest homes, a residential area with a lot of green."

Mark mused. "I'm beginning to see our neighborhood as a little less modest. We're not like the Colony, of course, but, as the disparity between the haves and the have-not's in our society grows ever larger, I regret that too many don't have the chances we've had to improve our lot."

"That's what I'd like to offer low-income folk, better lots to build on. I've been sharing ideas with the Reverend Jefferson Douglas of the American Methodist Episcopal Church."

"I don't know him. And I don't know where that church is—in town?"

"It's west and south. You . . . you wouldn't probably walk that way. But he's important in his community and can help us."

"We not only have better lots on Water, Main, and a few other streets, we tend to label them as if they're national treasures. We were noticing as we walked today the signs that document our status. In addition to the original owners—Winston, for instance—we have university flags, car makes and models, 'don't tread on me' lawns."

Charlene chuckled. "I've fallen for some of that, replacing the painted tires and cement block garden borders of my youth with picket fences and elegant birdbaths."

"As a Midwesterner," Mark noted, "the yard markers remind me of the old shaving cream signs along country-crossing highways back in the 50s. 'Don't take that curve / At sixty-per./ We can't afford, to lose / a customer. / Burma Shave.'"

"Now those were entertaining," Cathy agreed. "Each phrase printed on its individual board and spaced 100 yards apart along the highway, so you read serially. More attractive than the huge billboards that dominated the roadways beginning when . . . ? The '60s?"

Mark said, "That sounds right. Lynda Bird, as First Lady, campaigned to keep them farther away from the road. It's sad our highway signs today carry only one message: "Buy, buy, buy!"

Charlene concluded, "Well, the advantage—another advantage—of living in a small town is that you can make changes more quickly than in an urban environment. For instance, before the railroad was built here in the 19th century, there was a ferry service that crossed the river along the same route. You can still see some of the old pilings where the dock was. It could be transformed into a small neighborhood park on the river's bank."

"I didn't know there was a ferry," admitted Mark. "But I guess that would have made it easier than going west around all the swampy areas. There should be historic markers explaining forgotten parts of Staffordshire's past in sections of town not officially labeled 'historic.'"

Charlene agreed. "What's also interesting to me about the past is how early settlers brought in supplies and carried out local products—tobacco, lumber, peanut oil from the mill. The cargo boats they used are fascinating."

She pulled out another piece of paper with the blueprint of a boat. "They split one of the large cypress tree trunks in half, hollowed the two sides out, then joined the halves to a center plank that included a shallow keel below along the full length of the boat."

Mark noted, "That wouldn't draw much water, so it could

navigate shallow creeks, maybe even move into swamps."

"Yes. It's a common design used up and down the coast in the 17th and 18th-century. Cornelius Vanderbilt employed a version of it in a ferry service between Staten Island and lower Manhattan. They were replaced by steam boats in the North, but the Southern version was used longer. There's a reconstruction of one down Ocean Highway east of Staffordshire; but, because there's an admission fee--'donation,' they call t-- it's visited mostly by people out at the Colony."

She continued enthusiastically, "Now, if we townspeople put in a small riverside museum—free, of course—along here . . . ," she pointed to where she'd drawn in the bridge, "it could be a tourist attraction."

"Perhaps," Cathy added, "small shops, a restaurant, along with signs highlighting the area's past."

"Nothing big," cautioned Charlene. "The goal, as I see it, is to bring young working couples to town, helping them finance homes that would be great for families."

Mark was still studying the picture of the boat, called a "periauger." He said, "It appears to have both oars and sails—two masts."

"Yes, upriver, when there's little wind, a crew of six would work the oars—well, the 'sweeps,' as they were called. Long and heavy, so rowing was hard work. But, oh! the periauger makes a grand sight on open waters! The gaff-rigged sails—four corners rather than the more common three—provide enough power to pull the weight, a cypress trunk being heavier than a lapstrake hull. All in all, it's an impressive sight, especially on those rare occasions when dolphin are in the river, leaping out of the water and splashing back in as they swim alongside."

Cathy smiled. "It appears that, for someone recently moved to town, you have plans for the place."

"What I would like to see is more opportunity, especially for young people who might be encouraged to stay in town rather than move to the city. Some options and the freedom to choose. To get a college education and have a career, I had to move away."

Cathy wrote a note on the calendar they kept on the counter. "Count on us for the town meeting Monday night."

When their neighbor had gone, Cathy sat down at the kitchen table to total houses and potential guests from their survey, while Mark went upstairs to his study to consider possible invitation designs.

On his computer was an image he'd saved from a 1930s poster advertising Staffordshire. It featured a sailboat breaking waves and coming right at the camera. A woman straddled the bow; a small flag was at the stern. She resembled the pin-ups painted on the fuselages of airplanes in World War II. It was labeled "A boater's delight!" It was a provocative picture. Her blond hair blown back in the breeze, her red two-piece swimming suit bright in the sun. Her right arm reached down between her legs to hold the tip of the bow, and her left arm trailed behind her, turning her bare (white) shoulders at an angle toward the viewer. There was no bowsprit, but men would likely imagine one there.

He had an idea for the invitation. "Open water, open sky/ Bring Fourth," with a patriotic image to catch the eye.

Chapter Eighteen: Rooms

Coming down from his study, he saw Beverly with her handy-woman hands on her handy-woman's hips studying the Nelsons' garage. There was a small window boarded over above the double doors. "Do you want to restore the old hay hoist to get things up to the loft?" she asked Mark.

"I hadn't thought about that. Right now, we only have the trap door opening inside at the back. It's not big, and going up the step ladder with anything heavy isn't feasible. That's why I like the idea of a simple set of stairs along the back wall."

"That will work, but the hay hoist would give you a second method of getting stuff in and out. And the triangular support and pulley would add to the authentic barn look. It would be nice to have it ready for Bring Fourth."

"Well, I'm not sure that's necessary. I wanted to keep the, um, costs down."

"I think your wife wants it. You know, it's quite likely this building kept horses originally, as cars weren't common in the early twentieth century. So, hay or feed might have been stored in the loft. I'll take a look."

Mark followed her inside, wondering why, if Cathy had said she wanted it, Bev had bothered to ask his opinion.

"There's a lot of junk up there," he said, "and with starlings regularly freeloading on the space, you'd better wear a mask to keep from asphyxiating." He watched her disappear up the step ladder into darkness.

He's only looked in the loft once himself, just to survey whatever miscellaneous junk had been left up there by previous owners. He and Cathy had bought the house "as is," having received an assessment from a reputable local firm confirming that it was structurally solid. They figured they could lower their offer enough to make it a bit easier on their retirement finances, even if it meant taking time later to clear out clutter.

From the top of a step ladder, Mark had noted heavy metal buckets likely used to haul tar (given the dried black gunk on the rim) for sealing chimney flashing or other gaps in the roof. There were some old, decaying, window shutters, probably original but replaced when vinyl siding was installed. A set of cabinets was stacked in one area, which he assumed had been taken out when the kitchens was expanded through the closing off of the screen porches.

He had found much the same situation in the attic, which was easily accessible by a staircase on the second floor. At the same time the kitchen was expanded, closets were built into the second-floor bedrooms; and leftover lumber was scattered here and there. Closets were uncommon when the house had been constructed, and clothes were kept in large wardrobes. Several of those were stationed like guards close to the stairs. An old toilet, sink, and clawfoot bathtub were also tucked into one corner.

There was only a crawl space beneath the house, as basements in land barely over sea level wouldn't have been feasible; so, at least that didn't yield more things to be carted away. Still, there were cement blocks, old timbers, and rusted cans of paint in areas where he didn't want to crawl. As far as he was concerned, they would stay there indefinitely.

Reviewing all this, he and Cathy concluded that the Winston House contained its own past in odd spaces within the modified structure. A British colony before the American Revolution (Jamestown was less than two hours away), the town preserved it past also: English names (like "Staffordshire") for roads, waterways, and estates, as well as Anglicized terms of the native Weapemeoc.

Pieces of a centuries-old order were still occupying space into which the Nelsons had retired as, during the Civil War there was little fighting in the area, and Reconstruction preserved the agrarian social structure to which slavery was essential. The town didn't promote industrial development to move with the times, though, and the local economy was slowly failing.

"Here's something you might use for the party," Beverly called down from the loft.

Mark went to the back of the garage and looked up through the trap door space. "What have you got?"

She pulled the end of a pole, perhaps five inches in diameter into view. "It's either a flagpole or the mast of a small sailboat. Wooden, probably just a sapling that was straight enough to serve the purpose. And it's got a small pulley at the small end."

"That might be a way to advertise the celebration, flying a flag or banner. Can you get it down?"

"Not through this space—it's too long to stand up vertically. That's another reason to open up the loft window so we can get it out of here."

Again, Mark mused that reasons to employ Beverly seemed to simply appear. "Anything else up there of interest?"

"It's hard to see. There's a walled-off space in the front I'm curious about. But that can wait until we get an easier way up and down. I'm going to make some measurements for the stairs.

Mark went back to the house and learned that that he had been tasked with getting cider donuts for lunch, not as manly a mission as rebuilding a garage. He didn't ask, but assumed Beverly would share in the meal.

As he drove, Mark concluded that two conflicting forces had shaped the American identity: an Old World desire to establish a permanent structure for the generations to come; and the frontier impulse to pack up and head west, starting all over again. The Nelson family approach derived from his grandfather's emigration from Sweden.

At least he stood in a much shorter line at the Whole Donut Van today than in his first visit. "What's for you this time, friend of the Firecracker?" asked Douglas.

"Huh? Oh, you mean 'Fireworks Tom.' Yes, he was in line with me the last time I was here, but I'd never seen him before."

"Seemed to me the two of you were close. School mates? Fellow vets? Maybe kindred spirits?"

"No, no. He's just offering to do something for July Fourth in our neighborhood. Anyway, can I have a dozen of your best?"

Again, Mark observed the scars and tattoos that covered almost every inch of his skin. "So, how long have you been doing this . . . uh, circuit up and down the coast?"

"Since I dropped out in my last year of architecture school. Felt I needed to experience the open road and never went back."

He was using a pair of tongs to drop fresh donuts into a plain cardboard box.

"Ah, so, you might have been building homes but became a nomad, a traveling salesman, as it were, without a home yourself."

"Oh, I have a home: it just travels with me." He gestured at the beetle parked in another space. So, if you're not the Firecracker's best buddy, what do you do? I believe this is the first summer I've seen yo."

Mark handed him a twenty. "Retired. For many years public affairs officer for a chain of small banks in Virginia. And now a happy resident of Staffordshire."

"The Winston House suits you and your wife. Are you getting to be friends with the Lees? They're one attractive couple, aren't they?"

A few more customers were pressing up to the window, so Mark just took his change, shrugged, and moved off.

It suits us? He asked himself how that was. Was this an architect's view of how he belonged in a two-story frame house backing up on the water?

And why did everyone in this town—and even the occasional visitor—know his business before he did? Why did Douglas assume he and Cathy were friends of Randy and Caro-*lyne*? Even after more than four decades living in the South, he at times still thought like a Midwesterner.

Midwesterners and Westerners, he believed, valued autonomy, which generally meant keeping your doings to yourself. They also wanted few restrictions, a trait passed down by their ancestors who'd fled the more settled East. Those in the older states—the Northeast and particularly the South—accepted limitations created by tradition.

He had a foot in both worlds. Coming from a family that

bristled at notions like "It takes a village to raise a child," he'd gradually adopted a sense of community that bonded Southerners to their place. He'd fit himself into the Winston House rather than thinking to convert it to a structure suited to his history or personality.

What, he asked himself, were the values of his neighbors that had shaped the annual July 4 celebration in the past and what might any changes he and Cathy add to the community's vision of itself? Could he open up a new level of consciousness in the body politic just as Beverly would open up the loft of his garage? If so, his campaign would need an eye-catching invitation.

Chapter Nineteen: Bees

Mark sat near the back at the town meeting where options for replacing the Short Bridge were to be discussed. Cathy had stayed at the house to put away dishes after dinner but would join him soon

"You got any bees?" whispered a man who sat in the row of chairs behind him. Whispering was, perhaps, what he aspired to; but his voice was raspy, high-pitched, and it carried. "Or know where I can find some?"

"Um, no," Mark said over his shoulder, noticing that several heads had turned his way at the sound. The meeting hadn't started, but he assumed the man would be quiet once things got going.

"You just can't find 'em these days," the man complained. Mark realized this was the voice of a smoker. He could also smell the tobacco. "When I came back, I put up six hives and could have had more. I have over two acres with open space along the shore, which bees like. It's too swampy to farm, but I don't need no money."

"Ah," Mark agreed. He was tempted to ask, "Came back from where?" but didn't want to encourage conversation with the beekeeper.

The man continued anyway, leaning forward so that his head was just over Mark's right shoulder. "I've got one hive left. Don't know what's killing them, but I'm betting it's pesticide or herbicide. You know, like Agent Orange."

Mark had followed discussion of the herbicide used widely in Vietnam, informed by his doctor at the VA in Norfolk that he should be checked regularly for skin and prostate cancer; and he should watch his sugar intake to avoid diabetes.

Curious, he took a quick glance to his right and saw a face wrinkled with age and scarred from what he assumed was severe teenage acne. He also seemed to be twitchy, his hand on the back of the chair beside Mark lifting, his fingers gripping.

Mark gestured toward the podium at the front of the room, where the mayor was beginning the meeting. Members of the town council and two representatives from the state department of transportation were seated around him.

The beekeeper did lower his voice somewhat but didn't stop talking. "Everything's changed since I grew up here. Big farms worked by giant tractors; that fancy country club development on the Sound putting in invasive ground cover and electronic insect killers. And Sandy Point--man! Who knows what the hell they're up to! Biological or chemical shit is my guess."

Cathy came into the room with Randy Lee just as the men from the transportation department began showing slides and discussing possible bridge designs. Was it just a coincidence that his wife and Caro-*lyne*'s husband arrived at the same time?

When she sat beside him, Mark tried to make hand gestures in his lap to indicate she should not encourage chatter with the man behind them. He jerked a thumb to indicate behind him, and wagged his forefinger back and forth to suggest negativity.

The presentation went as Mark expected: the need to replace the old bridge, which was deteriorating and polluting the river; the importance of respecting town history represented by the Short Bridge; and minimizing the impact on the community. The truth was, he suspected, that the state would make the decision and claim it was what "the people" wanted.

His chatty neighbor occupied more of Mark's thinking. It seemed this man took him for a fellow beekeeper. Why? When the slide presentation came to a pause, the man tapped Mark on the shoulder and whispered, "Meet me in the hall."

Afraid he might create some sort of disturbance if he didn't go, Mark whispered (he really did whisper) to Cathy that he would be right back.

The man was standing by the water cooler. Again, Mark noticed jerkiness in his stance and his gestures. "Bees do good in cypress swamps, you know. They live in hollow places in the trunks. Without 'em, your cotton, your soybeans, nothing would make crops. Pollination, you know."

Mark nodded. "If that happened, all of Staffordshire would be in trouble. Not much else is profitable around here."

"Bees need open space, freedom to travel. Now, you could have a hive down by your bulkhead, if you put fencing around to keep anyone from bumping into it."

"I'm sorry, but I don't recall that we've met. How do you know about the Winston House?"

"Oh, I know all the houses on Water Street. When I was growing up, I'd boar down here, check out all the places from the water."

"You lived farther downriver?"

"I was supposed to be coming into town for supplies, you know. We didn't have a car . . . well, or electricity or running water, in fact. The family was off the grid, you might say."

"I see."

This didn't completely surprise Mark. His appearance was . . . well, rustic. And there was a bit of a smell. "Well, listen, I need to get back in to hear what others have to say."

He was also remembering how Beverly had indicated there were some "genuine characters" in the area where she grew up. This was probably one of them.

The man raised a hand in a "stop" gesture. "I understand you're a bit worried about the knees in your lower yard—you know, the knobs that grow up from cypress roots. Make sure you don't chop them down. They're important to the trees. And to my people."

"'Your people'?"

"The Weapemeoc. We were the main tribe in these parts when your ancestor invaders came." He chuckled and slapped Mark on the shoulder.

"Mine were later immigrants. But I understand what you mean."

"Yeah. We were like the bees, bringing a lot of things to

life in these parts. We took our open spaces for granted back then, being able to go where we wanted, but always treating the land with respect. Cypress knees told us we had connections to the earth."

He came closer to Mark, acting conspiratorial, though his voice, even in a whisper, traveled across the foyer.

"People think this country was founded on freedom, giving everyone the chance to go after their dreams. But really, it's the opposite: this country was built on taking away freedom. My people had good lives here before we were invaded. We knew our way around the rivers and the swamps and the cypress knees and the forests. But as you moved in, we got hemmed in. Some went west, but most of us just crowded into smaller and smaller spaces."

"It's a sad story, to be sure."

Again, Mark tried to turn toward the doors of the meeting room. But his new friend maneuvered between him and the entry.

"What bees do when there's too many of them, some go off to find a new home. A swarm, you see. If they don't find a place, they die. And it happened to many of my ancestors. My own folks, though, they were tough. They held on to their two acres despite never having a deed or a piece of paper to show they owned it. We don't ask nothing of nobody, living off the land and the river."

"That's commendable," admitted Mark.

"Sometimes we help someone, mostly for free. Other times we need a bit of cash, just to be able to function in white society. That's why I thought I might offer my services on the cypress knee problem before you host the July 4 event."

"Ah." Another challenge to face! He guessed, though, it was remotely possible this man had ideas passed down among "his people" that were worth considering. So, he nodded and listened.

"People always think of the knees as getting in the way," said the beekeeper. But really, they've got it all wrong. Folks are the ones in the way of the cypress; trespassing is what it is. They were here first, so we should learn to go around them—on land or in the water. You see?"

"Well, sort of. But how would this help us use our lower yard?"

He squinted at him. "You need to mark out a maze with them, —not 'maize' as in corn, now—but paths between and around them so that you don't bother them and they don't bother you. See what I mean?"

"Ah. Yes," nodded Mark.

Looking over the beekeeper's shoulder, saw Cathy push open the meeting room doors enough to raise one hand and, first, wag her finger at him and, second, crook it to say, "Get in here, now."

Chapter Twenty: Request

Mark sat at the small desk in the upstairs study, gazing out the window and hoping to refine the party invitation on his computer. "Bring Forth," he thought. It seemed like a call to action. But go forth to do what? Lift a glass and down a beer? It had to be more than that.

Producing invitation copies would be easy with the current technology, the laser printer he and Cathy shared. It was so much simpler than the process he'd followed at Jenson and Sons Printing years earlier. But he did have to come up with the right image.

Back then his boss designed images on a polymer coating, which he applied to a plastic or metal plate. It was offset by transferring the image onto a flexible sheet (rubber) for printing and publication.

The process of producing a final product was satisfying for Mark, but he was sometimes distracted by shoptalk with his boss and intrigued by the tales of Jimmy Hardcastle, a full-time employee. Mr. Jenson would visit his station regularly, lingering to talk about the weather, baseball, the state of the nation. "Hot week ahead, I'm afraid," he'd say, apologizing in advance for the lack of air-conditioning in the building.

"The fans help a lot," Mark would respond, glancing at the small unit on a metal stand directed at him and his machine. A huge exhaustion fan in the back wall blew hot air into the alley behind.

"We're lucky, though," Mr. Jenson explained. "The bank across the street blocks the late afternoon sun. And there are plenty of hotter places around the world than where we are, that's for sure!"

As he listened, nodding his head from time to time, Mark was also daydreaming about his campaign to woo Veronica. At college the previous year, he'd found himself naive compared to the big city kids; but he planned to play the sophisticated college student back home that summer. Jimmy Hardcastle had outlined a scheme for him, claiming he'd used it to score with many girls. ("I score with more," he boasted.)

As he recalled those events, Mark at times found himself

substituting for Veronica the figure from the "boater's delight," the poster advertising Staffordshire' charms. A two-piece was as close as you could get to risqué swimwear in a small 1960s Midwestern town.

Jimmy outlined the spiel Mark was to use with Veronica. He was supposed to say, "I don't think there's any harm in my getting to second base. You don't want to be a freshman in college without a certain amount of experience." It would turn out she had plenty of experience warding off hands that strayed and words that swayed.

Still, one Friday night Mark proposed (as Jimmy advised) that they squeeze through the fence around the municipal swimming pool and swim nude ("the way they do in Europe"). He offered to go first. ("Pants down. / Game on," was his unspoken motto.) Soon Mark was splashing around in the shallow end of the municipal swimming pool—closed, of course, at that hour—and beckoning Veronica to join him.

But then Mark saw her back on the other side of the fence, his own swimming trunks held aloft as she slipped away into the dark. "Pants down; / Pants gone," she wrote on the back of the putt-putt golf scorecard, which she left in his bicycle basket. She had ridden her bike to a friend's house several blocks away. Mark never found his trunks. He concluded he'd put too much faith in the printed words he imagined on signs, the medium of Jenson's Printing.

He came to admire the more skeptical attitude of his sister Isabella, two years younger. She had also learned their father's guidelines but was skilled at evading them and establishing her own rules.

She might hesitate on the threshold of 412 Elm Street, then act as if she'd forgotten the doorway rule. "Go where?" she would respond innocently to her father's instruction of

"Come in or go out." On their way to church, a solemn duty, she would suddenly ask, "Was I supposed to make up my bed?" The rule was "Wake up and make up." She also concocted her own gently mocking principles: "Sleep tight" became "Teenage Sleep is Twelve-teen Hours."

Their hard-working and patient mother accepted her family of strong personalities and provided a neutral but nurturing presence. She would find her husband studying the bank statement as if it were an arrest warrant or a summons to court: "All Payments are Due." And she would lure him into a game of checkers, with its simple rules but complex patterns: "Crown me. / Jump you."

She would pull Isabella aside and remind her that her father had grown up the only son of a Swedish carpenter, who'd arrived in this country with $15.00 in krona and the address (incorrect, it would turn out) of a distant cousin penciled on a page from the New Testament. Mother told daughter, "Be patient; / Be kind."

Mark would sometimes call his time at Jenson and Son's "the summers of maxims and pranks," entertaining friends with versions of what he'd done—sprinkled with fairy dust. "Be All You Can Be," he reminded his listeners, borrowing the deservedly successful Army recruiting slogan and suggesting he'd been all he could have been.

Not that he didn't become successful, taking advantage of the economic booms of the '90s and pursuing a chosen career. Truthfully, though, he'd speculated about building up a printing company, modeled on Mr. Jenson's but more expansive and more refined. And the words "Don't Ask" came to haunt him at times of self-reflection.

"Why the two signs?" he'd asked his boss late in August, perhaps thinking he should understand before leaving for

Westminster in a few weeks.

"They don't teach history anymore?" answered Mr. Jenson. "What President made this statement? 'Ask not what your country can do for you . . .'"

"Ah, Kennedy."

"Yes, the man who inspired your generation but didn't survive the anger."

"So," Mark puzzled it out. "You're not saying, 'don't ask,' then; you're saying don't ask for things. Ask what you can do. Well, JFK's dreams got tangled up in LBJ's war, didn't they."

Mr. Jenson sighed. "Yes, and so did mine."

"Your dreams?"

"My son answered the call, wanting to be like his dad." Mr. Jenson had newspaper stories of his WWII service on a bulletin board in his office. "Oscar died in Vietnam, a hero." He took a deep breath. "But Kennedy wouldn't have given up, so neither will I. I want us all to ask what we can do to help each other here and abroad."

With the innocent confidence of youth, Mark was sure he would be doing that after he finished college. When he was older, he came to see how much more he could have done outside outside his professional career.

He could hear Beverly and Cathy downstairs studying the map of Staffordshire's Water and Main Streets, counting up likely guests for the 4th. He wanted the flier he was designing to do more than invite everyone to a party. It was a celebration of the nation's founding, an appreciation of principles that, he hoped, were still guiding the country. But why couldn't it also be an articulation of how those principles should guide us into the next 100 years. "Bring Forth" our best.

He recalled Charlene's concern that the status quo put some neighborhoods with no way to improve. What image could he put on the invitation that might nudge neighbors toward change? Washington crossing the Delaware? Lincoln's stern face at Gettysburg? Susan B. Anthony arrested for voting when women did not have that right? Martin Luther King declaring "I have a dream"? Kennedy, hair blowing in the winter wind at his inauguration: "Ask not what your country can do for you"?

No, all that was too heavy. He smiled at "A Boater's Delight," but chose instead an image of a dolphin shooting straight up out of the water. "John Smith" had claimed it as a symbol of freedom. He concluded it was inspirational and underscored the words, "Bring Fourth."

A few days later, however, when Cathy turned those words back on himself regarding his commitment to their union, he would feel he'd not been all he could have been.

Chapter Twenty-one: Gravity

"You wouldn't mind if I pulled a quarter of your ear, would you?" asked Raymond, who'd appeared behind Mark out of nowhere. It was the day after the Nelsons had sent out the official invitation to Bring Fourth.

Before he could finish saying, "Excuse me?" the hand of his one-time garage guest swept past the side of his head and came around in front of his face, a thumb and finger pinching a shiny silver quarter.

"Oh, the old magic trick," Mark chuckled. "What's next, a

rabbit out of your hat?"

Raymond stepped back a pace and pulled off his Army boonie hat. He bowed, put his hand in the cap, and took out his hand, a furry bunny dangling by its furry ears. "Not real, my fried," he assured Mark. "Lots of groups complained about the trick when it was a live rabbit, so I've had to use Bonnie's . . . great-grand-niece, I think she is . . . her stuffed toy."

He and Mark were in the side yard of the Winston House. Mark had been pulling out the snap beans and preparing the soil to plant bush beans. Raymond had snuck up on him from the front of the house.

"So, you're a . . . professional . . . magician?"

"Yes, now and then, here and there. I do kids parties, the occasional bar mitzvah, a quinceañera in some parts of the country. Depends on where I am, you know. But I've never registered as a business or gotten a vendor's license. Off the grid, you see."

"I do see, unofficial, like a hobby." Mark also foresaw that Ray was going to propose entertaining at the July 4 event. He would have to head that off. "Do you saw people in half? That's a pretty impressive trick."

Ray shuddered. "Not my thing. Saw some bodies come apart back in the war. You might have seen that, too. So, no."

"Sorry, didn't mean to bring it up. How about making things disappear? You made a quarter come out of nowhere . . . well, out of my head, I guess. So, have something vanish into thin air."

Ray smiled. "Now, that I can do with my lovely assistant. And here she comes."

Mark turned to follow Ray's nod and saw Cathy walking toward him from the back of the house with three steaming cups of coffee and three donuts on a tray.

Mark smiled. "She's always been magic to me. But I didn't know she also worked with you."

"Come back to the screen porch," Cathy said. "We can talk more comfortably."

She would explain later that Ray had come to the front porch, rung the doorbell (the one Bev had fixed), and offered whole donuts if she'd make whole bean coffee. "Mark's in the garden," she'd told him.

"I'd prefer your lovely assistant not disappear," Mark told Ray. "But you've been invisible yourself for some time. On the road?"

"Yes, I have. Went to see an old friend, my Donut Dolly, if you will."

"One of the Red Cross ladies who came to cheer us up in Vietnam like in earlier wars. Unsung heroes in my book. So, you're talking about one in particular?"

"Let me tell you about her in a minute. I want to enjoy this coffee and the cider donut." He took a bite and a long drink of the coffee.

Mark was pleased to smell no alcohol on Raymond. He told him, "I don't know what kind of magician's assistant she is, but she has always made good coffee."Cathy smiled and Ray agreed. "I believe that. But, you know, the future of coffee makers isn't that bright compared to what a magician's assistant might enjoy."

Cathy winked at Mark. "Tell me. Maybe I'll want to explore a new hobby."

"You see, here's the thing. Magic is the line between light and dark, day and night, here and there. The magician's hand is free to make things disappear and appear, be present and then absent. And he takes the audience with him."

"And she takes them" corrected Cathy.

Ray chuckled. "'She.' Right. Of course. So, what I'm thinking here is you and me might want to experiment a bit with an act, see if there are ways we can transport others out of the daily frame, open up their lives to things they didn't see before."

Cathy nodded, but she also frowned. "Now, I'm not interested in casting spells, hypnotizing, hallucinogens. Sleight of hand is one thing, but mind-altering tricks . . ."

They all knew what she was talking about. "No beer or wine," insisted Ray. "No coke or acid, none of that. Maybe a few hidden mirrors, an unseen trapdoor, gestures that distract the viewer while you slip something up your sleeve."

"Ah yes," sighed Cathy, "some of the ways we could liberate others from the prisons of perception."

Ray laughed. "Now I like that phrase: 'the prisons of perception.'" I can see it on the side of our van, along with "Winston, the . . ."

"'Winston the Conjuror'?" offered Mark.

Cathy added. "What about and 'And his lovely assistant, Katerina'?"

"You're getting ahead of yourselves," said Ray. "Let me tell you about Dolly."

"You mean a Donut Dolly?" asked Cathy.

"Yes, but also Dolly. That was her name, so I always called her Dolly Dolly. I met her at a USO club in . . . Pleiku, I think it was. She could sing, dance, a born entertainer. And she'd even done a bit of magic back in college."

Mark wondered, "After college she served with the Red Cross in a war zone?"

"She dropped out of the University of Florida where she was a cheerleader for the football team and a straight A student. But Dolly Dolly felt the call, you know, to buck up our spirits up over there. She was Tina Turner doing 'Proud Mary.' Did someone cheer you up in 'Nam?"

Mark chuckled. "Lola Falana. But at a distance. She was with the Bob Hope Christmas show, and I was a hundred yards away from the platform. But she could sing, and her hips could rock the back row."

"I know what you mean, brother. Dolly Dolly could do the same. I asked her if she liked to be my lovely assistant, and she said maybe."

"Weren't you assigned somewhere?"

"I was doing a bit of . . . um, recuperating in-country. Unfortunate incident . . . somewhere I can't remember. But I had one arm that worked pretty much and two legs. My head was a bit messed up, I'm afraid. Anyway, Dolly Dolly pulled a quarter and a dozen demons out of my ear, and I began to get better."

Mark nodded. "And your act? What did you guys do?"

"Levitation was our best. She'd lie on this cot, I'd wave my hands, she's float up in the air—no strings attached. (Well, none you could see.) We overcame gravity, the strongest force in the universe. It keeps the moon from flying away, the planets in orbits."

"But you free us from that force?" wondered Cathy, almost wanting to believe.

Mark recalled riding helicopters in Vietnam. You felt extra G's going up, but sometimes weightless in descent, floating.

"Magic can take away gravity," insisted Ray, "but only temporarily. "We're always drawn back to earth." He sighed. "Especially, soldiers."

"So right," agreed Mark. Cathy could see they were moved.

"It's crazy, man," Ray said. "But I go back to the good times more and more these days. Me and Dolly, well, we had good times."

"It's a goofy nostalgia," agreed Mark. "We were surrounded by so much . . . shit. Sorry, dear. But the good times can still lift us up."

Raymond took Cathy's hand and pressed a quarter into her palm. "Magic, Dolly. There it is."

"On another matter but also about a veteran," Mark mused. "Do you know a local guy, calls himself 'John Smith' and says he's still does, um, 'contract work' for the government?"

Ray rubbed his chin. "Old guy? Well, a senior like you and me?"

"Yes. Maybe even older than that."

"Slim, wiry looking, like he gets regular exercise?"

"That's what I concluded. Could have been Navy or Marines."

"Living downriver some, not in town?"

"Right."

"Serious but smiley, too?"

"Exactly."

Ray shrugged. "Nope. No one around here like that."

Chapter Twenty-two: Eras

At the next Friday afternoon gathering on Anne-Harriet's screen porch, Mark, recalling 'Dolly' Dolly, Ray, and John Smith, saw a chance to direct attention to how none of us escapes the current of history. He would argue that a July 4 celebration should be seen as step toward the future rather than an escape from the present.

The hostess had raised the issue of change in Staffordshire customs, referring to the town meeting on the Short Bridge. "Did any of you think it was a bit odd how many questions the Lees, the couple that bought the little store on Main, asked?"

Vickie nodded. "Things like: 'Do absentee landowners have a say in this discussion?' 'Is signage included in the plans?' 'Who makes final approval on the project?' They're newbies who are pushing their way forward in town affairs." The word "pushy" was a strong one in this crowd.

Mark had, of course, shared with Cathy the strange conversation he'd had with Mrs. Lee (a possible double of *The Americans'* Elizabeth Jennings). His wife didn't take it any more seriously than the suggestion that the Simpsons' grand-daughter planned to accept "contributions" toward her college fund in return for "favors." They had decided to stay quiet about the idea of a drug boutique operating in the next block. With the John Smith episode they realized they were now keeping a number of things from their neighbors.

Patrick was tolerant of the Lees' questions. "Oh, they're just big city people, measuring investment and return, opportunity and risk. They'll settle in . . . just like Mark and Cathy." They smiled. But that was when Mark sensed an opportunity to explore the potential of Bring Fourth.

"You know, I walked down to the old bridge the other day, imagining what the site was like in earlier eras. Wasn't there a floating bridge there before this one was built?"

"And a ferry system before that. Transportation has gone through stages over the years."

"Well, that reminded me about a bitter-sweet encounter about boats we had, oh, twenty years ago. Cathy, you remember Trixie, the steamboat museum guide."

"Oh, my, yes," she said, wistfully. "Trixie. You might even say she saved our marriage."

This was an exaggeration, but she knew Mark would approve of hr helping to launch (so to speak) the tale. Despite its setting in a place of storage (a museum), the story of Trixie always had a surprising restorative effect on the present.

"You two took one of those Caribbean cruises?" asked the pastor.

"Not exactly," admitted Mark. "Not nearly so exotic, though beautiful in an odd way."

"Europe, then, down the Rhine or out of Gibraltar?" asked Vickie. "Growing up in the war and after, I didn't get to see the magnificent castles and towering cathedrals."

Cathy said, "Again, sorry. We didn't even leave the country."

Anne-Harriet suggested, "The Alaskan inner waterway along Canada?"

Mark confessed, "No. You're all being too romantic. We toured the Howard Steamboat Museum in Jeffersonville, Indiana, right across the Ohio River from Louisville."

"You mean you went down the Ohio on a restored boat from the Mark Twain era?" offered Patrick. "Now, that would be interesting, so long as the boiler didn't blow. They had a lot of accidents back in their day."

"Yes," agreed Mark, "but the Howard ships, built by European engineers, were meticulously put together. Every piece where it should be, built to the most precise requirements, fitted together as tightly as a jigsaw puzzle. Engine, controls, instruments—built to last."

Cathy explained. "Actually, we didn't get on a boat, just took the tour in the museum. But I have to say a journey back into the past became a ride toward the future. And it protected us from the explosion we were headed for in our marriage."

"It was," Mark admitted, "a time of stress for us—the two jobs, the children in high school. We were kind of cracking at the seams."

He didn't want to admit that this last month getting ready for July 4 had generated a similar tension in their relationship. While this was a much less stressful situation, he and Cathy were considerably older. And though he felt the anxiety more, he knew she had had moments of doubt also.

"We're not the only couple to face this kind of professional and personal challenge," admitted Cathy. "But then the tour guide became an unexpected inspiration for us."

Mark laughed. "And an unlikely one. She might have been the oldest person on the staff, or in the town, or in the state! But the name on her badge, clipped precisely on her lacy collar, was incongruously 'Trixie.'"

Cathy explained. "The young woman who sold us our tickets said, 'Trixie will be right with you,' so we expected some high school student or an undergraduate to come skipping through the door labeled 'Staff Only.'"

"But tottering out was this tiny, tiny lady, using a cane, thick glasses, blue hair so thin her scalp showed through. 'Let me take you on a voyage to the past, my young friends,' she announced, 'to the fine world of expert workmanship and refined behavior.'"

"Now," Mark chuckled, "she was speaking to the room in general, peering this way and that, because I don't think she could spot us exactly through those thick glasses."

"And this is the one who saves you?"

"That's what happened," nodded Cathy, "though at this point we're trying not to roll our eyes at each other. I'll tell you this, though: her Victorian outfit was meticulously put together—the nineteenth-century dress, the hair brushed into place, bright red lipstick, rouge cheeks, mascara eyes. How she kept a steady hand in dressing at her age was a mystery!"

Mark continued. "She led us into the main entrance with its grand staircase spiraling up to the two floors above, family portraits on the walls, gingerbread decor. 'Travel, you know,' she told us, wagging a finger in the general direction of our voices. 'Travel can free you from convention. Give you a new start . . . a new start.'"

Cathy said, "That was when a shadow seemed to cross her face. We didn't know why at the time, but we would learn later in the tour."

Mark thought of John Smith who had reminded him that his sailing on the Persimmon River helped him take a fresh look at his problems. While early steamboat passengers had been moving to different places in the past, today's river tours still meant taking a break from the everyday, considering changes.

He went on to explain how the 1894 home, built by master steamboat craftsmen, contained eloquent furnishings, brass chandeliers, stained glass windows, and intricate carvings. Each room featured a single wood: cherry in the dining room; pecan in the library, olive master bedroom, walnut library, bedrooms in teak, oak, ash. The floor, fireplace, and mantel (wooden cased mantel clock, as well) matched the tables and chairs, the bookcases framing the windows, even the pianos, pianofortes, and spinets. A nautical compass was set in a wooden box on its own small shelf by the door.

Mark also noted that the floors were the most striking part of the construction, as the boards ran diagonally from corner to corner, not side to side. 'That's the way they're done in a steamboat,' Trixie lectured us. 'The triangle is the strongest geometrical shape. The diagonals are the right angle's hypotenuse, the walls are the adjacent and the opposite sides. You see, the river waters put such stress on the whole structure, it has to be extra strong.'"

Anne-Harriet asserted, "Anything that's going to last has to be well-constructed."

Cathy agreed, "Yes, by this time, we thought we were getting over our bad start . . . or at least I was, nodding appreciably at each of her comments, asking questions. And you were trying, dear, pointing out that the garden off the dining room must have hosted many a wedding reception."

Mark laughed. "But Trixie scolded me sharply, 'We don't allow that' and led us across the hall to see the Howard's great desk. But there were photos of outdoor receptions in the garden with bridal parties in white. We had no idea then what had set her off so strongly."

Cathy winced. "We tried hard to be appreciative, but, after our first faux pas, we couldn't recover. 'Don't touch the musical instrument,' she said. 'Did you wipe your shoes before coming in? We don't like . . . dirt . . . in here'—as if we were the mud!"

Mark admitted, "Oh, we did more to earn her criticism, though. Once it was because I felt compelled to help. She was going to take us up to the second floor, and I was concerned she'd trip and come tumbling down the stairs. When I asked if there was an elevator, Trixie snapped. 'There were no elevators in 1894.' And she started up the stairs, ignoring the banister, and I tried to put a hand under her elbow."

Cathy said. "She was blunt. 'Excuse me, young man. I've been going up and down stairs since before you were born.'" She shrugged. "Now that seemed to me the opposite of a qualification for the task."

Mark smiled. "And it was worse when she turned midway up the first flight to point to a faint line that marked how high water from the river rose in the flood of 09.' We were sure she'd spin free from us down the stairs, her cane clattering after her dry old bones to the mahogany floor below. But, no, she balanced on the step and reminded us how well-built the mansion was, surviving flood, storm, and time."

Cathy sighed. "It was on the second floor that the truth came out."

Chapter Twenty-three: Green

"Boom!" shouted a voice from the sidewalk. "Fireworks Tom ready to talk flash and bang with Mr. Mark."

Patrick looked sternly at Thomas Beard. "He's . . . busy here. Come back another time."

"What! Having a beer on a Friday afternoon? That ain't busy. I've got an idea of how to make this the best Fourth of July ever."

Mark apologized to the group. "It will be easier if I just step out for a bit." More softly he added. "And I need to get this over with."

Vickie insisted, "You'll have to finish the story of Trixie, though."

Cathy assured her. "If we don't get to it this afternoon, we'll schedule a back-up date with dinner. And I want to tell about our leucistic cardinal, as distinctive a creature as Trixie that's been coming to our feeder for the last few days. It's white where it should be red, a result of a rare gene mutation"

Patrick nodded. "I've never seen such a bird, but I did see an albino alligator in a swamp over by the Alligator River."

"Where else would one be?" joked Anne-Harriet. "And I do think they should stay on their side of the Albemarle Sound." The river was perhaps 35 miles from Staffordshire as the crow flies, but the drive around rivers, swamps, and the Sound would generally take over an hour.

A decade ago, after news that the species was spreading northward because of climate change, the fear of alligators snatching pets in residential lawns or mauling people in streams or rivers had taken hold of this community. Any story about an attack on a human (most of which occurred in Florida) made the Greenville and Norfolk evening news.

Patrick said, "I'll give you a positive view of the Alligator River that involves birds, but not leucistic ones. The highway 64 bridge over the river is a gathering place late in the summer for purple martins preparing to migrate back to the Amazon. Birdwatchers from all over flock," he paused to emphasize the pun, " . . . flock to see the thousands of birds who've come down the East Coast. They wait there until the conditions for travel are right."

Mark smiled. "I'm amazed at how things so small can travel—it's nonstop, isn't it?—from here to Brazil."

"It doesn't seem physically possible, but hummingbirds do it, too. Annual migration is a natural phenomenon," added Vickie. "The expression 'free as a bird' means something in this context."

Cathy added, "We're happy to think of our martins joining that group. It's the third year for our house, but the first in which it's been occupied."

"I've always loved the deep purple of those birds," said Vickie. "It shines in the sun."

"And they eat their weight in mosquitoes!" smiled Patrick

Mark heard about this conversation later, of course, after his exchange with Fireworks Tom. Cathy admitted it was the

kind of wandering discussion that characterized those in Darlene's.

Mark and Tom had walked across the street to survey the
July 4 party location. Mark worried that he wasn't going to
survive the proposals Fireworks Tom would bombard him
with. But the town character surprised him.

"I've got something to beat the Colony's Independence
Day display," began the possible descendant of pirates.
"Ready to hear about it?"

Mark wondered if one-up-man-ship might be a reason to
do without fireworks. "Hit me," he said, then added, "Not
literally, of course."

"So, here's the deal. We've always known that fireworks,
just like guns and other things that create explosions, can be
bad for the environment and bad for us. It's not simply common sense but science that tells us this."

Mark wasn't expecting him to take this approach. "Yes,"
he agreed.

"You see, nitrates, chlorates, and per-chlorates are widely used as oxidizers in fireworks. Potassium nitrate, for instance, was once an ingredient in gunpowder recipes. But
sodium chlorate is a popular herbicide often added to home-
made concoctions."

"To have fireworks, though, don't we need these ingredi-
ents?"

"Maybe not. And let me also remind you that these things
also create health risks."

Again, Mark nodded. "There's certainly pollution—bad for
people with respiratory diseases, skin issues, hearing sensitivity."

They walked down the bank toward the bulkhead, surveying the water, which was completely calm. "Interestingly," Tom continued, "the US military has been looking at alternatives, seeing as their weapons have the same effects. Now, any new chemicals in explosive devices need to do three things: 1) generate the traditional bright flash; 2) resist taking on moisture; and 3) be stable enough not to go off accidentally."

Mark asked, "And they've found . . . what would we call it?—'green' materials to make weapons with less flash and boom but still effective?"

"Sort of. What they talk about are innovative—green, if you will—oxidizers. The idea is to use smokeless charges and sulfur-free propellants. The consequence for us is that there are now fireworks following the military's example, though they're not easy to find around here."

"That doesn't surprise me," said Mark. "And if we could get some, they'd be more expensive that the traditional kinds."

"Right. There's no easy way to have a truly green fireworks display, but we could try to get the word out that we're doing something new with fewer harmful side effects. I might put whatever the Colony does in a different light."

"Hmm. It would be worth the extra expense to get at least a sampling of these new things."

"Take a look at this list of ways to reduce the hazards of fireworks."

Mark scanned the sheet, which he immediately saw could be integrated with his Bring Fourth publicity. The list, put out by a group called "Bomb Lite," recommended using noise-free ground fireworks, especially if you suspect bird nests or other animal burrows where you set hem off. You should watch the skies for birds like osprey and bald eagles when you launch aerial devices. Check weather forecasts to time your display when the wind is blowing away from neighbors. And advertise what you're doing to local authorities.

"I like this. And you think the Colony is not going in this direction?"

Tom chuckled. "Oh, no. They want what they do to be seen and heard far and wide. And the only way to do this right now is with traditional fireworks."

"Okay. See what you can get to justify our declaring a 'green' Fourth. And I'll do research to find out what else we might do."

Cathy, who'd never met Tom Beard, was surprised to hear of his proposal. "It would be a small step to have a green celebration," she told Mark. "But, to go forward, we're going to have to take a lot of small steps."

"I think we can make a statement, if a modest one; but it might change a few minds about how we live these days."

"We were talking just last week about bomb shelters and the fear of a nuclear Armageddon back when we were children. Now, more nations have bigger and better weapons. There are local conflicts that could become global. And there's climate change. Despite the fact that you and I have had a good life, it makes me mindful of the fragility of our existence."

"And we do think about the next generation—not just our own children and grandchildren, but their friends and counterparts around the world. If the purple martins can't make the trip up here to have babies—chicks, I guess—they wouldn't be anywhere next year."

"Our cardinal made me think the same thing: a genetic mutation caused by environmental factors could occur. A leucistic bird may be more vulnerable to predators because they don't have the species' regular protective coloration. I also read there's a chance that the feathers are not as capable of shedding water and protecting against cold as those of other birds. If cardinals lost their coloring, we might have no more beautiful red—or white—birds brightening our days!"

"Or, if our underwater surveillance guy—John Smith--fails in his mission, submarines will come up the Persimmon River and take us all out!"

Twenty-four: Doves

"So," said Beverly to Mark as she stepped down the stairs in the garage. "So, do you want the doves to be released at the party; and, if so, would it be okay to launch them from our new loft window?"

Several things disturbed Mark about this question. First, how did doves even come up among possible elements of Bring Fourth? Second, if the idea had been discussed, was it in another of those exchanges between Bev and Cathy they had deliberately kept from him? And third, how were they supposed to pay for the mounting expenses he was beginning to learn about—patriotic decorations and paper goods, fire-works, music, now doves of peace?

"Doves, white doves, I assume. Is such a thing done each year at the party?"

"Oh, no. This would be a first. But I understand you want to impress the neighbors. And it's a pretty amazing display—plus no sound, but wings; no light, just feathers. An impressive display of freedom."

"You've seen it?"

"Oh, yes, my cousin has them. She doesn't use doves, but pigeons. Doves are a fragile bird, actually bred as pets. They're not likely to survive being freed in unfamiliar territory. Pigeons, now—to be precise, Linda uses rock pigeons—will generally fly home (she lives downriver). Even if they don't, they're adaptable and can settle in new places, even in cities."

"I see. So, so they're homing pigeons. I like the idea, but it's bound to be expensive. And is it fair to the birds? We don't want a SPCA person bringing charges for cruelty to animals."

"Linda does her homework. It will all be legal. We can play 'Let Freedom Ring' as they take to the sky. Of course, weather can be a factor. And we need to schedule this when fireworks are not going off—early in the day, even before Big Bob fires up the grill."

"'Big Bob'? I thought someone delivered a grill, and we did the burgers and hot dogs."

"Oh, yeah. Cathy and I realized the Robinson's grill isn't really big enough for the crowd we're expecting. So, I contacted Big Bob. He lives outside Harbor City and runs a catering service. He's got what we need. He'll truck it down the day before."

"Ah." (More costs!)

"Now, the regatta . . ."

"What? We're not arranging a boat procession, surely!

"Nah. Just playing with you. I wanted to see your face when I brought it up."

"Ho-ho. Well, one more thing on the pigeons: you're sure

they all make it home after the display? I've only heard about one or two birds released by the owner. Even in World War I, when they were used to carry messages over the front lines, it was a single messenger, not a flock."

"Yes, a flock would have been noticed. As it was, the Germans did catch on and alerted their troops to take down any flying creature. It was yet another part of war's devastation, although small overall. So, talk with Cathy. We still have a few days to contract Linda."

When she was gone, Mark climbed the stairs and surveyed the space above the rafters in the garage. The loft window was still boarded shut, so the space was dark, confining. He thought again of Harriet Jacobs, an enslaved person, spending seven years unable to feel the sun, to communicate with family, even to stand fully erect. He, a white man of privilege, was fretting at having to host a party in a prosperous community!

Even racial tension seemed less now than in the past, though Latinos, Middle Easterners, and immigrants in general had to earn respect, whereas native born citizens assumed it. Mark wondered about the resentment surely building inside and outside the country that could threaten the nation's belief in its exceptionalism.

How little had Southern plantation owners and the businesses dependent on them known of the Underground Railroad? What exceptional individuals suspected that there was a social network linking Southern slave quarters to safe houses to the Northern free states? How many saw the signs of revolution coming?

It occurred to him that local black ministers at, say, the American Methodist Episcopal Church, might know more about this part of local history than the residents of Water Street. He could check the Staffordshire library as well, small though it was.

He thought of the cypress knees in his yard, connected to roots intertwined with those of their neighbors. He recalled the beekeeper's assertion that, if you understood things correctly, the knees created pathways for travel, not obstacles. And bees, of course, flying miles from hives to flowers to hives charted the ways of vitality.

Pigeons, too, revealed processes of connecting. He hadn't mentioned this to Beverly, but he knew a bit more about one variety of the bird. Tumblers are bred to perform gymnastic maneuvers—to tumble.

When the Nelson family took a summer vacations to visit Western landmarks, he'd spotted a poster advertising "The Amazing Tumblers of South Dakota." The sign caught his attention because there were birds pictured in a variety of positions: right side up, right side down, curled up in a kind of ball, wings spread wide almost like parachutes.

The pigeon show was to occur in Wall, South Dakota, which was where they stayed while visiting Badlands National Park. He showed the family the poster. Cathy asked him if they "tumbled" on prairie grass or cliff tops or main streets.

Louis, at 15 ready to pretend to knowledge on any subject, said, "They probably set up a stage, what you might see at a carnival. It's a touring performance."

"Wherever it is," asked Mary, 11, "Can we please go so he has something to do."

Louis was demanding she play with him and his Game Boy. Although she enjoyed doing so with her girlfriend, she refused to acknowledge that the teen obsession held any attraction for her.

Mark's understanding of tumbling pigeons was changed when he watched them perform. They didn't do so on the ground, but in the air.

Their owner released them from cages stacked on the back of his pick-up truck. They rose in circles above the parking lot and the prairie grass hills beyond. At a certain height, some of the, perhaps a quarter of the flock, dropped out of the group and fell toward earth. They did not slam into the ground, but after executing some remarkable aerial gymnastic maneuvers, spread their wings and rejoined the larger group.

Their descent was swift and varied: some birds did somersaults, head over heels, others spun along the axis of their bodies like bullets pointed directly at the earth, and some looped and circled in a variety of moves. While there is no agreement about the purpose of this tumbling, the tendency is genetic; and pigeon enthusiasts have deliberately sought them out. These birds may simply need an occasional rush. Or they have an unusual metabolism and need to burn energy to participate in the group's regular activities of eating, nesting, and breeding.

Tumblers were bred in the Middle East more than one thousand years ago. The practice spread to Europe, where the birds became valuable property, traded and bred to become entertainers or pets. Individuals in many countries today of course, keep pigeons as a hobby and may own gymnasts as part of their brood.

Watching the birds perform in Wall, Mark chuckled at the idea that some humans are tumblers, too. Appearing to conform to social standards and practices, they suddenly drop out, spinning out of control to a surprising location. At some later time, they rejoin conventional society, no worse for the journey. Beverly, the lawyer/handy-woman struck him a possible tumbler.

He thought of his fellow Army correspondent, Bruce, who slipped out of officers' sight to pursue his own goals in Vietnam. Because the sense of mission there had become unclear by 1970, slack in the system provided opportunities for GIs in the rear to hide. Troops in the field, of course, did not enjoy that luxury.

There were gaps in the social network of Staffordshire now, too. Even on traditional upper middleclass streets, there were houses in need of repair—rusting metal roof, sagging porches, shrubbery gone wild. Welfare had become a way of life for some, passed on from generation to generation. A few dealt drugs on a small scale, providing alternative "employment."

Mark also realized that there are groupings of animals, including humans, that go unnoticed or unknown by most of us: tumblers among all pigeons. Thinking of his guest list, he wondered which could be called "patriots" in a traditional sense—displaying flags, supporting the armed forces (often with a military past or family members in the service), believing in the ideals of the Founding Fathers.

Others would call themselves patriots, too, but these "tumblers" reject the slogan "my country right or wrong." Ideas of the Enlightenment should, they argue, justify spreading rights to groups historically left out of the nation's freedoms—women, persons of color, people with non-binary gender identities. Could the two kinds of patriots (and, of course, there are other definitions of the term) coexist, cooperate, and collaborate on a future that evolved as they pursued it?

Chapter Twenty-five: Rats

When they joined the usual group sharing cocktails on Anne-Harriet's porch Sunday, they were pressured to explain their plans for the Fourth. "Remember to keep an eye on the Simpson granddaughter," insisted Vickie. "She's a smooth operator."

Cathy replied, "Beverly has agreed to be here, and we've alerted her."

"But she's mostly supervising set-up," Mark reminded her. "We're not sure how long she'll stay in the party."

"Your children are close, aren't they?" asked Patty, the pastor's wife. Cathy had learned—at Darlene's, of course,—that she was often gone for weeks at a time, visiting family, it was said.

Cathy sighed. "I fear they're occupied where there are, up in Chesapeake. But we're planning to be watchful ourselves. You know, block parties can be more than simple celebration. Folks talk about what's going on in their lives, what worries them, and what is encouraging. We don't want to feel that we're a secret police circulating among the people."

"We liked your invitation: 'Bring Fourth.' It's . . . cute."

Mark had not included the plans for a green fireworks displays, deciding to save that for a reminder flier that he'd distribute a day or two before the Fourth. There were climate change deniers in the group, and he didn't want them to boycott the event. And he didn't want to tip off the Colony of his revolutionary display.

Cathy explained that Mark wanted to have a theme. "When he formally welcomes everyone, he'll also say what he thinks the slogan means. He's going back to Trixie, our steamboat museum tour guide."

"I'd like to lighten up the story by minimizing mistakes we made with our docent," admitted Mark, "but I'm afraid I have to take responsibility for the biggest blunder of all."

Cathy explained. "There was a beautifully crafted model of a steamboat in the library, The Union, built by the Howards in 1888. It was so detailed that it took Trixie more than twenty minutes to describe every feature on the deck. It, too, was constructed with many different types of woods."

"Back then, cruises probably spread disease also," Pastor Baldwin noted. "The 1918 flu epidemic was a global one because people could circumnavigate the globe."

Cathy didn't respond. "Trixie did know her material, our docent, explaining the engine and the paddle wheels, the staff quarters, the kitchen and dining rooms. She identified the wood and the style of the furniture in the big rooms, the portraits in oil hung everywhere, the eloquent meals served three times a day."

Mark agreed. "She pointed to brass chandeliers, stained glass windows, and intricate carvings throughout the boat. Even the insides of the cabins were perfectly scaled with minuscule furniture, hanging brass lights, ashtrays made of seashells, and tiny human figures doing what they would on a cruise."

"Newlyweds on their honeymoons?" asked Vickie with a nostalgic smile.

Patrick arched an eyebrow and smiled. "On their wedding night, then, in the deluxe stateroom, its canopy-covered bed with satin sheets."

"Trixie's lecture was hardly R-rated," laughed Cathy. "But you hit on a key point: today's popular culture makes us all seek out the lurid detail."

"And the skeletons in the closet," admitted the reverend. Cathy noticed that this wife's eyebrows went up when he said it.

Mark sighed. "Well, Trixie's narrative may have been idealized, but thinking back now, and seeing it through her eyes, it was a picture of serenity."

"And we blew it," admitted Cathy. "We had to notice the little lifeboats perfectly secured at the model ship's edge. They were ready for any emergencies."

"And, peering through one of the tiny portholes," nodded Mark, "I had to say under my breath, 'I think . . . I think I see a rat abandoning a sinking ship.'" Cathy looked sympathetically at her husband. "Trixie heard him and echoed mournfully, 'A rat abandoning a sinking ship.'"

Mark confessed, "And at that moment her face just came apart. Lips started shaking, cheeks sagged, tears smudged makeup so that, while still connected, the elements of her appearance lost their relationship to each other. 'What did I say?' I asked myself."

There was a hush on the porch, drinks on the way to lips paused, dip scooped onto chips froze, gazes stayed focused on him; but it was Cathy who spoke. "Mark looked at me, and for the first time in the whole experience, I think we shared the same feeling— sympathy for our ancient guide, Trixie."

Mark looked at her and smiled slightly. Then he said, "Her jaw fell and mouth opened as if some sound—a sigh, a cry, a gasp—was coming; but it didn't. As her forehead wrinkled, the sparse hair above it seemed to become even more immaterial, a blur of selfhood floating away from a source. Where

Trixie had been standing, it seemed that all we could recognize was a dissolution."

"My God, what caused it?" asked Vickie, concerned now, too, for a person she'd never known. "Heart attack? Stroke?"

Cathy explained. "I put a hand on her arm. I asked her what was wrong, what could we do. She straightened up and said simply, 'He left me.' Her voice was coming from somewhere deep inside her, or almost from a soul . . . that had already gone on to another life. 'After 62 years of marriage,' she wailed, 'he just walked out, declaring himself a free man.'"

Mark said, "Even after her critical attitude toward us, it was hard to hear, hard to watch."

"They'd married when he came back from the war," explained Cathy. "They'd created a life together—a home, children, grandchildren."

"Sixty-two years! That's not possible," claimed James. "What did we call that generation, 'the builders'? They started businesses and had families, children. They stayed together in good times and bad."

"I know," agreed Cathy "But at that moment, it seemed to us that the end of her marriage was the end of an era."

"Of course, as we all know," concluded Mark, smiling at his wife, "that there was an end to the steamboat era. The railroad was coming, to be followed by the automobile, the airplane, the space shuttle, the future."

"What will follow the present" wondered Carl, making the discussion even more sober.

Cathy lifted her glass. "Whatever the future will be, when we come together this Independence Day let us commit to building wisely and well, as the journey ahead of us is long and the hazards many."

They all murmured agreement and clinked glasses. And, fortunately, Patrick launched into an amusing account of a local man who, may years ago, tried to mount the engine from a Stanley Steamer on a crab boat. It sank but jokes about Stevens' steamed crabs surfaced in many later conversations.

That evening, putting out left-over lasagna and a salad, Cathy said, "Well, our story of Trixie took on a negative tone. But I'm committed to 'No Negativity.'"

"Well, we put ourselves out there: 'No try, just do.'"

"Yes," agreed Cathy. "I guess we were trying to . . . oops! We were celebrating . . . her ability to hang in there. When we've told the story to younger people, it seems more distant, about others not them. But with our senior seniors this hit home more than we anticipated."

"I still find it ironic—Trixie correctly telling us travel—real or imagined—can change how we view things. Her husband traveled; he moved on."

"Well, about reactions, I've had some interesting ones to the invitation. Wanna' hear some?"

"None is going to best your 'Bring Froth (as in beer).'"

"I don't know. On the same theme, I have 'Fifths for Fists.' Charlene, a bit more serious, told me 'Forth for Bridge,' suggesting—not that we need get a fourth player for a game of cards—but that we need to get together with others with a plan on bridge replacement."

"That's good. And she's right about it. The town, not just the neighborhood, needs to figure out what would best for all.

There was also one negative note in our mailbox that read, 'Free Fi Foe Dumb.'" He spelled the last word so he could be sure she understood.

Cathy frowned. "So, '"Free-dumb.' I'm guessing that's from someone who thinks we've extended the 'rights of man' beyond what was intended by the Founding Fathers, there being, of course, no founding mothers."

Mark shrugged. "It's clear democracy is an unstable ship with a rebellious crew."

Cathy looked hard at him. "I want to be sure our union, you and me, are a stable ship. Are you getting over the anxiety July 4 was causing you? If not, I need to know."

He hesitated. "I think I'm okay, though I still have some ups and downs. Sometimes 'Negativity' bushwhacks me."

"Try to remember: 'Ask Not.'"

Mark knew he'd sometimes been thinking of himself more than Cathy, his neighbors, or the town, asking what they could do for him. He came back to the idea of a special anniversary event. To match what was now unfolding at Cathy and Beverly's hands he might need to have a blimp fly over trailing a sign, "Mark Loves Cathy Over the Moon."

Chapter Twenty-six: Bear

When a brown bear lumbered down Water Street the following week, Mark was not surprised. He assumed this was one more participant in Bring Fourth who was making demands: perhaps honeycombs hung in all bushes; berries in tubs; tree trunks to rub against and satisfy itches. "FunForFur."

Of course, that was not the case, but it was a happy illusion for a moment. Then, like everyone else on the street, he panicked. He raced from his small garden in the side yard (where he'd been tying up his tomato plants) to the back door off the deck and locked himself in the house. Cathy was in the kitchen freezing more of the peaches they'd purchased at the orchard west of town.

"Bear!" was all Mark could say, and that breathlessly.

"I hope this isn't one of your come-ons—bare your breast or backside. I'm busy blanching peaches. Later today?"

He would reflect that evening that he was a lucky man whose wife offered herself in response to a one-word announcement. But right then he wanted her to be aware of bear, to stay inside, even to avoid appearing in windows and doors.

Wishing he'd never wished for a wild creature to wander into his life from the Great Dismal Swamp, he hurried down the hall to the living room, closed the blinds, and stepped over to the parlor to do the same thing. He hoped the bear would conclude no one was home at this house and proceed to break into a home where lunch was being served.

His mind raced over what he'd heard about the free roaming creatures of the Dismal Swamp, asking himself if this was worse than an albino alligator coming across the Sound to visit a playground. He decided it wasn't, but still . . . .

The black bear (Ursus americanus) is large. Later he read that, at 4-6 feet in height, their average size is 250 pounds, but they can weigh as much as 600 and run up to 25 miles per hour. And they can both swim and climb, so no escape on ground, in water, or up trees.

Mark's general conclusion of the moment was that this ambler might crash through the door, climb in a window, eat a couch as a snack. It was the answer to the old riddle of where the 800-pound gorilla sits on an airplane—anywhere he wants to.

"Who do we call?" asked Cathy, who'd cut off the stove, put aside the pan filled with peaches, and followed him to the front with cell phone in hand. "Wildlife Control?" She typed in the words. "There is one! I'm calling." She tapped the link and put the call on speaker.

"You have reached North Carolina Wildlife Control. Please listen to these options, as they have recently changed."

"Push zero," said Mark, "And keep pushing zero until you get a living person . . . or maybe Smokey the Bear." He'd learned this shortcut to a phone message system on the Internet.

Before she heard a live voice, a recording announced, "If you are calling about a brown bear in the town of Staffordshire, we have been notified and are on our way to the scene. Stay inside your home or business. The bear will smell food in your garbage cans or storage sheds outside and be occupied with whatever he finds. Do not, under any circumstances, approach the bear. He's a wild creature who can be dangerous."

Mark slanted the venetian blinds in one living room window just enough to peer out at the street. Ursa Major had knocked over the garbage bin that his neighbor had put out last night for today's collection and pawed the contents into a pile. He was squatted down plucking out trash that he considered edible—the package that had held hamburgers, eggshells too slow to break down in compost, an empty container of canned apples.

Mark looked around for Wildlife Control—or any uniformed person—but saw no one. But wait! From the direction of town came a man wearing a long shirt not tucked in and carrying what looked like Gandalf's staff in *Lord of the Rings*. It was his friend, the beekeeper.

Mark hissed to Cathy. "Psst. Come here. The guy I told you about—from the town hall meeting. It looks like he's taking on the bear."

Mark reasoned that Ursa Major came from the swampy land on the north end of the causeway and followed his nose across Short Bridge into town. Beekeeper probably traveled from downriver and moored his boat in some out of-the-way place, like the back of the episcopal cemetery, three blocks south of the Winston House. Tall cypress blocked the view from the river there, and bushes at the back of the cemetery did the same from the street; so, his transport was safe.

Mark could see the man's lips moving. Was he chanting? Perhaps he was drawing on the wisdom of "his people" and using a special language the bear would understand. What could he be saying? "Nice bear, nice bear. Please go home now." No, that's something his granddaughter might try.

Cathy took Mark's elbow and looked out at the scene. "The question I have is does beekeeper see the two bear cubs meandering along behind their mom?"

Mark saw them now, too; and a flood of stories about people being mauled when they inadvertently got between mother and cub surfaced from his memory. He was frozen in place, fearful that a shouted warning might antagonize the bear, leading to an attack on beekeeper or himself.

Beekeeper remained calm, however, and slowly raised his bamboo stick to his mouth. Was it a blowgun? Did he have a poison dart to paralyze Yogi? No, it was making a sound, flute-like. The bear paused and cocked his head. Beekeeper took another step forward.

Mark noticed he made none of the jerky motions he had noticed at the town meeting in the courthouse. His movements were slow, controlled, easy.

Astonishingly, the bear sat down slowly in front of beekeeper, his head still slanting a bit to one side as he gazed at this stranger with a long stick. Music calms the savage beast? His eyes locked on the man in front of him; he rotated his head in a small circle.

Beekeeper lifted one hand, palm down, then lowered it. The bear leaned forward from the waist, almost bowing as if before a deity at a shrine. The man repeated the hand gesture, and the bear slumped over on one side and lay still.

"What the . . . ?" whispered Cathy.

"Oh," said Mark as he saw a man and a woman in brown North Carolina Wildlife uniforms carrying rifles emerge from behind some bushes across the street. They must have fired narcotic needles into the traveler from the Great Dismal Swamp and her two children. It was not the chanting beekeeper.

"You saved the day," he told Cathy. "Calling Wildlife Control."

"Well, I wasn't the only one. And I think I'll give credit to the agents for this one."

Watching rangers retrieve their agency pickup truck and, with a lift, hoist the sleeping bears into the bed was anticlimactic, but the Nelsons were hypnotized by the process. When the truck had driven away, they saw neighbors coming out to their sidewalks to share their accounts of what they saw.

Mark and Cathy went the other way, deeper into the house. She stood at the stove, not moving the pan of peaches or turning the burner back on. She just stared. Mark walked over to the kitchen door and looked out over the deck to the water where John Smith had waded ashore only a few days earlier.

"What else is going to happen in this town between now and July 4? An invasion of clowns, a stampede of wild buffalo, a traveling rodeo setting up on the high school football field?"

Cathy responded. "I have no idea, although, since we've had strange visitors come on land and by water, I think you'd better look to the skies for what comes next. But you want to know what my first and second thoughts were about the bear?"

"Of course. My first thought was WTF. This is the Swamp Monster ready to imitate King Kong in a place much smaller than Manhattan."

"I can understand that. But I thought at first this is just some publicity stunt, a guy wearing a bear suit. It's a promotion for, I don't know, a car dealership or an insurance company. Pretty soon he'll pull off the head of the costume, tuck it under his arm, pull out a bullhorn—or bear-horn—and announce. 'Great deals now at Large's Cars—new autos, previously owned giant trucks, riding mowers as big as Humvees.'" Large's was a dealer in Harbor City.

"Ha! Maybe I should hire someone to wear a kangaroo suit and a Bring Fourth sign on his back. But your second thought?"

"You won't like it because it's been your feeling all along. but the way the unexpected keeps happening, I wondered if we may need to be thinking of a back door out of hosting this party."

Twenty-seven: Agency

Mark went out to talk with the beekeeper, who had remained standing where he was when the bear had collapsed. "You were mighty lucky out here today," he offered.

His advisor on beekeeping and cypress knee navigation smiled and asked, "How so?"

"Well, the Wildlife guys. Did you know they were there?"

"I figured they'd show up at some point to claim credit for capturing a wild bear."

"But they shot him—her—with tranquilizers. Otherwise, you'd be chopped liver—literally. Those two cubs, she would have done whatever was needed to protect them."

"So, that's what you think? The agents knocked out the beast with drugs?" He came over to stand closer to Mark. "My friend, that bear—'Piemacuum' to my ancestors—went to sleep because I sang to her, a song as old as the river and the cypress with their feet in her water."

Mark didn't know what to say to this, so he just nodded. Then he noted, "I don't think I ever got your name, back there at the town hall meeting."

"Beverly," said beekeeper.

Mark's face showed surprise. "You're 'Beverly'?"

"No, I'm Beverly," said a voice behind him. He turned to see the "handy-woman," who then said, "Hello, He Who Travels Well."

The beekeeper—apparently his name was "He Who Travels Well"—put a hand on her shoulder in some kind of formal greeting akin, Mark surmised, to a handshake. "We are well," he said to Beverly, who, Mark guessed, might have an entirely different name to him—She Who Climbs Stairs or Writer of the Law and Sweeper of the Floors or Back up Bear Tamer.

Now Cathy joined the group, smiling at the attorney/handy-woman and the beekeeper/friend of cypress. Mark stepped back to let her direct the conversation. Both the reality of a bear on Water Street and the language used to describe the event had been cut adrift from familiar moorings. He felt he was floating above the scene.

Cathy said, "Whatever happened out here today, we're grateful no one was hurt."

He Who Travels Well leaned on his bamboo pole/musical instrument. "People tend to overreact when a free animal enters the grid of streets, property lines, buildings."

Beverly smiled. "You and I have seen all sorts of critters in town besides the usual possums, skunks, raccoons, snakes, turtles. When we have drought, the river gets salty, and you can even see dolphin chasing white perch right up to the bulkheads."

A mermaid on one's back? wondered Mark. It didn't seem too strange now.

"Of course," laughed He Who Travels Well. "Osprey, eagles, turkey buzzards, hawks, and owls don't have to walk or swim to show up in town."

Beverly nodded, "Sometimes the whole river slips out of its banks. And we witness the usual panic whenever Mother Nature overrides boundaries."

Cathy seemed interested. "My understanding has been that, because the land is so flat in Tidewater, streams and rivers don't exactly flood; they just spread out a bit more. There are no stable banks keeping them in a channel."

Beverley nodded. "That's right. It's high winds that can drive water violently—storm surge. Your yard has had its eastern edge pushed back by hurricanes; and owners brought in soil to restore the old bank. What you see right now is not a permanent arrangement."

He Who Travels Well agreed. "Folks put up bigger and stronger bulkheads, call for government help when their fields are too wet to sustain crops or their roofs fly away. Better to build with an eye to change, not constancy. Right, Charlene?"

Mark startled. Their new neighbor had come up behind him so quietly he hadn't been aware of her. The landscape was shifting again.

"Yes," said Charlene. "We need to be ready for shifting shapes—or as they sometimes sing in the Navy, 'Our brethren shield in danger's hour, / From rock and tempest, fire and foe.'"

Those words made sense to Mark, as one of their ministers in Virginia had been the captain of a nuclear submarine in the Navy before deciding to retire and pursue the ministry. So, Mark, hearing this song (not He Who Travels Well's music), concluded that he might be coming back to firmer ground on the day Ursa Major came to town.

To steer the conversation toward topics and language he understood, he asked Charlene, "Maybe we should suggest that the replacement for the Short Bridge have a feature which would keep bears from invading—a cattle-guard, bear-bar, or something like that."

She frowned. "It could be one thing to consider. Right now, I'm concerned about another potential invasion."

Seeing more people coming into the street and cars crossing over from Main Street, Cathy concluded it would be hard to continue the discussion here. "Let's step around to our back deck and hear what you've learned. If we stay out here we're likely to be interviewed by the paper." *The Staffordshire Times* came out twice a week.

As soon as they'd taken seats, a pitcher of iced tea, two liter-size bottles of soda, and glasses appeared—Cathy's usual magic. Charlene took the floor . . . or the deck. "You all know the wind farms west of Harbor City—giant turbines stalking across the horizon."

Beverly frowned. "Some energy company purchased the Henderson farm, over 100 acres that's grown soybeans, cotton, corn, winter wheat for decades. Dusty Sherman told me farmers nearby are also upset. *Buff* is a small plane and can maneuver well; but those giants are in the way of his crop dusting."

Anne-Harriet added. "His trade nosedived," she winked, "when they went up."

Where had she come from? Mark hadn't seen her in the street, so she must have slipped in with the group as they walked down the side of the Winston House.

Aloud he noted, "Solar farms are also changing the landscape. Between Staffordshire and New Town and farther south and west they're spreading like wildfire—well, I guess that's not a good way to describe it. But alternative energy is quickly becoming a cash crop."

Charlene said, "I'm sympathetic to those who think the windmills are eyesores, mechanical monsters invading from the industrial north just like Union armies a century and half ago. And solar panels tilting to follow the sun—pointing east, up, west—seem like metal and glass soldiers goose-stepping in front of a podium full of military officers. But . . . but that's not an issue I want to take up right now. It's what may be following in their wake."

Mark chuckled, "So, you're not going to be like Don Quixote, taking up lance and sword to demolish the giants that were wiping out notions of chivalry?"

"No," Charlene laughed. "In fact, I'm going to take up arms against Don Quixote himself—or the projected Don Quixote Amusement Park."

Cathy asked, "There is such a thing?"

"There is in the minds of some corporate planners in the Northern Virginia/Maryland area. I've been researching property sales in counties around ours and learned that contingency purchases are in place for over a thousand acres north and west of Staffordshire. And the backers of this enterprise are working state officials to push the business highway so far west that you would have to drive three miles to come into town."

Anne-Harriet asked, "If Short Bridge was abandoned, and we wanted to go to places on the other side of the river—right now less than half a mile away—it would be a drive of four or five miles—east on the old road or west on this new one. We'd be cut off from old friends upriver on the north bank."

Charlene admitted, "Their plan is to build motels and cabins for visitors on the site, not here. They've been talking with real estate agents in Harbor City and Suffolk about where their employees can find housing."

Cathy said, "Staffordshire would live in the shadow of a ghastly theme park. People would come to take rides on Sancho Panza's donkey, chances to tilt against metal windmills, eat at restaurants modeled on medieval inns, wenches serving beer in iron mugs. Spare us!"

"Well, it's not a done deal—yet," said Charlene reassuringly. "But we're going to have mount a public relations campaign across town if we don't want to lose our identity."

Anne-Harriet mused. "I've begun to wonder what is our identity any more? We see so many new people—you guys are great," she said, nodding toward Cathy, Mark, and then Charlene. "But the folks out at the Colony, why, they're mostly . . . well, they're not Southerners, not North Carolinians."

Beverly offered, "We're not the old South, and we need to be part of the New South, which balances the new with the old, the modern with the traditional."

"And," said Charlene soberly, "the white and the black." Nodding at He Who Travels Well, she added, "The people of color."

Chapter Twenty-Eight: Rides

The man in the water, the bear in the street, the cheap versions of Don Quixote—a menagerie was spreading across Mark's mental landscape at the same time challenges to Bring Fourth were increasing. Even more than Cathy, he was asking himself, "What next?"

Over morning coffee the next day Cathy asked him, "Tennis, anyone?"

His response was "Huh?"

"I walked by the little store Caro-*lyne* and Randy Lee are fixing up".

"Okay," said Mark. "Did they offer you a joint?"

"No. She invited us for tennis. He doesn't play, but she's found a partner here."

Mark had played tennis regularly throughout his life, making number one his senior year on his high school team. He wasn't good enough for college varsity, but Cathy had been. They later they became a leading mixed-doubles team in a YMCA league.

While they hadn't been on a court together since coming to Staffordshire, Mark had convinced himself they were still capable as a doubles partners. To stay at least marginally ready, he sometimes stopped on a bike trip around town at the municipal tennis courts next to the senior citizens center and the one-room public library. He imagined finding someone warming up, and, as he'd done back in high school, he'd ask if he'd like to "hit some."

To take these trips for exercise, he had bought on old three-speed Schwinn cruiser at a garage sale that made him think of his rickshaw rides decades ago in Saigon, South Vietnam. He was generally successful in repressing memories of the nearly disastrous last time on a stolen bicycle taxi.

There were two kinds of rickshaws in Saigon: those with a two-person passenger seat on wheels pulled by a single man in front between two long poles; and the elongated three-wheel bicycles with the driver in back and a passenger cab out front. Many, though functional, could have used paint and better tires and had earned the informal label of "ricketyshaw."

"I wonder if I've met her partner," Mark wondered. "Did she give a name?"

"If she did, I've used my senior short-term memory to forget it."

"Remember how I told you that one time several weeks ago, when I stopped to hit off the backboard, I noticed a man standing by the library, watching me. He looked athletic, thin, average height. There was an expensive blue athletic bag at his feet."

She laughed. "And like a kid from your childhood, he asked, 'You wanna hit some?'"

"Ha! Exactly right. Well, he said his name was Lester or something and he had only been in town a few months. So, we ended up playing for an hour."

"The courts are underused, for sure," admitted Cathy. "Most, apparently, play at the high school. Didn't you tell me he was good?"

"He was very good. He had that slim athletic physique. His facial structure and skin color suggested he was Asian, Indian or Pakistani perhaps. Colleges, as you know, recruit tennis players from around the world. Let's see, what was his name? Les, Lester maybe."

"So, he took you to school, but was willing to consider playing again?" said Cathy.

"That's right. It was scary how easily he did it. He never hurried, placed the ball just out of my reach, glided over the court. Didn't miss a volley, and I felt he could have served much harder than he did. Hmm. If he's Caro-*lyne*'s partner, we're in big trouble."

"Thanks for counting me out! I may be older, but I still have some strokes. Now, you also told me what he did, but I forget that, too."

"I found out when he offered to do something for my shoulder." He gestured to his right side and rotated his arm, testing for soreness. "I told him that, when I haven't played in a while, it can act up. Goes away, though, as you know. But he suggested some exercises that would relieve the pain."

"But as I recall, he wasn't a physical therapist."

"No, that's the funny thing. A chiropractor, somewhat free-lance. He said his 'practice' was informal, one-on-one. Just coming to people's house saved him the expense of having an office."

"Aren't there problems doing that, with health regulations and so forth?"

"Yeah, but he doesn't take insurance, and that's where most of the restrictions come from. 'Cash works best,' he claimed; and he's free to adjust to each patient's schedule."

Cathy wondered how many clients he could locate in this little town. And Mark didn't answer, recalling the end of the informal tennis match, which he hadn't related to Cathy.

Les, or whoever, had said, "I . . . uh . . . walked over today, but I need to get out to the ABC store." The liquor store was out on the bypass, a little over a mile away. " Then he added with a chuckle, "I guess you don't take passengers."

Mark replied, "No, not on this old bike and at my age. Sorry. I guess you'll have to hoof it. There's no public transportation in our little village."

Les was surveying the library area, where a rack held bikes, most looking neglected if not abandoned. "I think I must just borrow one of these. Folks don't lock them in 'your little village.'"

He walked over to the library. "Hell, I'll just ride out, get what I need, bring it back. I'll put a note on it and say it was an emergency."

Before Mark could say more, Les slung his bag over his shoulder and a leg over the seat and pushed off. Mark was upset and, suddenly, very tired. He felt he was reliving that bad moment in Vietnam. And he didn't want to tell Cathy about that any more than he wanted to finish the story of the bike theft. He remembered it now.

Sam Barber, one of his fellow correspondents, had told Mark during his first weeks in-country, "You gotta learn to like Vietnamese food." They'd hitched a ride into Saigon for the day and could see GI's walking and riding in rickshaws—before curfew, of course. Mark naively assumed it was safe and went with him to Ec Phó, a narrow cafe off a side street in an area not frequented by US personnel. He had the Bàhn Mí pork sandwich and liked it.

Still, Barber kept a hand on Eddie's elbow in stretches of the half-mile walk to the restaurant and back. "There are some places along here you don't want to go. Right now we're in the red light district. If you want to make a visit, go with someone like me who knows the ropes."

A month later they went to a Saigon bar catering to GIs. The drinks were cheap, and attractive Vietnamese women in tight flowery dresses slid into the booth or onto the stool next to soldiers. "Want some company, GI? You buy me drink; we talk."

Standing in the street several hours later and swaying slightly from the drinks, Mark said, "We need to get back." Mopeds and little cars sped past. "But I don't see a taxi." He slapped his hip pocket. "My billfold's gone!"

"No use going back in there," laughed Sam. "It's long gone and empty. But shit, I'll get you back to the transient barracks."

He pulled up an abandoned rickshaw that had been leaning against a building, swung a leg over the seat, and said, "Hop in."

"What the hell," thought Mark. They took off, swerving into the traffic, ignoring shouts and the honking of squeeze-bulb horns mounted on handlebars.

It turned out Sam didn't remember where he was or how to get back to the compound. He went around a several block area looking for landmarks. When he veered into a poorly lit street, a group of young Vietnamese men suddenly blocked the path.

"Cowboys," hissed Sam. GIs were warned about these disaffected young Vietnamese, boys who rode Hondas, wore flamboyant body shirts and tight pants, and could be dangerous. America's support of democracy had given license to segments of Vietnamese society we had not anticipated.

"Your bike, GI?" one asked. "Or mine."

Shaking off the bad memory, Mark asked Cathy, "So, we play Caro-*lyne* and her unknown partner on what day?"

"Ten-thirty Tuesday. She didn't want to face the afternoon heat."

Mark responded, "Well, let's try to see it as one more way to get to know our neighbors." To himself he wondered if a real or imagined injury on the court could give him the chance to back out of hosting Bring Fourth.

Chapter Twenty-nine: Resources

Before the tennis, he and Cathy encountered another view of their environment that would add to his case for having a green Fourth and lessening the danger to flying creatures.

Reverend James Baldwin offered at that week`s gathering on Anne-Harriet`s screen porch. "This was not as a minister, though. It was . . . well, quite a few years ago, when I was an amateur chiropterist." He paused, clearly assuming someone would ask what that was.

"An expert on bats," Cathy volunteered. Seeing his face drop, she added, looking down. "I just learned the word the other day on a crossword puzzle." She was doubly embarrassed because the minister's wife, Patty, was with him today.

"I not only studied bats," the reverend admitted, "I kept some as pets."

Anne-Harriet mused. "I have known people who have birds, even owls, but not bats."

"Well, the pet project . . . " he paused to chuckle at the pun. "The pet project didn't turn out so well because the species doesn't tolerate being caged. They need to be free and active. But I also had a lot of bat houses in the back yard; and they could come and go from those as they pleased."

Vickie said, "I'm always afraid bats will fly into my hair when I'm under a street light." She did have beautiful hair, going to Darlene's regularly to have her "do."

"I've heard about that happening, but I don't know if it's true." Patrick noted. "I thought their radar guided them away from telephone poles, branches, things that could be harmful."

The reverend reassured them. "Bats are hunting insects at night, not people's heads. It can happen that one, chasing a mosquito or something, might run into a person, but that's really more of Hollywood myth than a real danger."

"What about wind turbines?" asked Mark.

"Now, they are a danger to bats as well as to birds. Back in my chiropterist days I ran an experiment. Around my quarter-acre back yard I built a miniature windmill farm. I think some of neighbors considered it an eyesore, but I wanted to observe. I was single then and had the freedom to pursue my whims."

Mark watched the other faces to see if this revelation about his past drew special interest. His narrative—a home with a sizable yard—suggested there had been an extended bachelorhood before he and Patricia met. But no one perked up.

"Like the engineers of giant mills, I put small lights on the windmill blades and installed a timer to alternate their blinking in such a way birds would be aware of them in the dark. Then I added discs that bounce the noise bats make back to them, reducing, or so I hoped, accidental collisions. Still, it happened occasionally. I kept meticulous records of victims, sadly burying my little mammals. And I tabulated the likely casualties in a full-size wind farm."

Sympathetic, Anne-Harriet asked, "Aren't bats like purple martins, eating up the mosquitoes we breed abundantly down here in our marshes and wet spots?"

James nodded, "Yes. Actually, these flying mammals save agriculture billions of dollars in pest control each year. Just like bees, they're very helpful to our farmers. But I assure you: these giant wind turbines are the single largest cause of mass bat mortality around the world. The cotton, soybean, and sage farms down here are bound to suffer over time."

"Now, that's serious," said Cathy, trying to make up for her earlier intervention.

James agreed. "Bats constitute one fourth of the mammal species on earth. They're gregarious beings, and their social organization makes them relevant to the study of human behavior."

"Did that lead you into the ministry?" asked Mark. "From bat colonies to church congregations."

James laughed. "It's not too great a leap. But I took an intermediate step into marriage." he smiled at Patty. She smiled back.

"You know," he continued, "bat pups are raised in maternity colonies, but the males have no role in that process. They have more to do, of course, in the courtship process. Some species of bachelor bats line up in trees along a riverbank and honk at nearby females to woo them."

James paused contemplatively, and Mark wondered if he was going to explain how he'd wooed Patricia. He also wondered if there had been a first wife, before her and the period of his bachelorhood. But the minister went on about bats.

"I learned more about species mating at a conference at the Blue Ridge Hotel in Virginia. Anyone else ever been there?"

Cathy smiled, "We spent a weekend getaway there. It's a neat old railroad hotel, built on hilltops with three wings along ridges. We found it's not an easy building to navigate. Hallways go off at odd angles, handicap-access ramps have been built through old closets and storage rooms, stairs are of varying heights, and signs are often confusing."

James again tried to suppress his displeasure at a significant part of his story being supplied by someone else. "Very true. I'll tell you about that . . . maze . . . in a minute. But first let me explain a different feature of the hotel. I found a nicely printed card on the bathroom towel rack that said, in large bold print, 'Save Our Resources.' Smaller print explained: 'Help The Blue Ridge Hotel reduce water and energy consumption by reusing your towels.' Such requests were becoming so common that I registered its meaning without reading beyond 'Save . . .'"

Mark agreed. "That happens all the time now. They shower us with slogans so much that we really don't pay any attention to them." He realized he might have overdone Bring Fourth.

The minister went on, "As I was hanging up the hand towel, I focused on the black marble granite countertop, a resource that apparently didn't need to be saved. But you know, they get a lot of that granite in South America, ship it to China for polishing, then transport it to America for sale with the idea it will last forever. The earth has only so much stone."

Patrick added, "So much of western Virginia's resources—like coal—have certainly been depleted in our lifetimes. I guess you were also thinking about saving the bat population."

"I was. But you're already guessing that I was moving toward my current profession—saving souls." He paused, perhaps a bit sad that he had to give this hint earlier than he wanted. "We each have only one of those, of course."

The listeners stayed still, so he went on. "I had found a good session about bats and the environment where I thought I could offer my thoughts. But I had to go down to my car for a book I'd forgotten, and, in that hotel of many corridors, I managed to get disoriented."

Cathy winked at Mark. She'd sent him out one night to

find a Diet Coke and gotten undressed to adopt a provocative pose on the bed. But he'd lost his way and was so long returning that she dressed and started reading a book. She still teased him about the surprise scenario she'd prepared and he had missed.

The minister continued, "Heading in the direction I felt the parking lot was—the opposite side of the building from the circular main lobby—I followed red and white exits signs and took whatever stairs I found going down. Some led to staff-only doors, others to patios and gardens (not parking), still more to long hallways with yet more exit signs at the end."

"Finally, I arrived in what appeared to be the building's basement. Passage was tight with steam and sewage pipesoverhead. Large floor polishers with handlebars and seats were randomly parked next to room cleaning carts. Brooms and vacuum tools angled up or sideways, and various types of liquids were stored inside compartments. But there were no signs for exit."

He said "no signs" with a dramatic air, satisfied that he now had control of the narrative.

"And just when I thought I'd better retreat the way I'd come, the lights went out."

"Ha," said Anne-Harriet. "You were a prisoner in a cave tunnel at a bat conference."

Again, James' face showed his disappointment with lines pirated from his story, especially as this came at his expense. "Now, this had happened to me before and deep inside mountains, but then I was always carrying backup lights and had studied the relevant maps. I memorized the route ahead of time and always filed a notice of my excursion with the appropriate officials. The basement of the Blue Ridge Hotel was unchartered territory."

Cathy, feeling that she'd spoiled some key parts of his story, said sympathetically, "And your past experience did save the day?"

"No," answered Mrs. Baldwin. "I did. I was assistant manager of room service and had come down to locate sheets for the honeymoon suite. It's how we met."

Patrick smiled. "I didn't see that coming, but it's a nice finish to your story, Reverend."

"I guess you could say she heard my honk," he said wistfully.

Mark wondered what kind of blessing this bat lover would have for July 4--offering liberty to citizens, birds, bat, and bees Maybe his wife would help him craft the message.

Chapter Thirty: Birders

Two days later, the Nelsons were coming out the front door with their tennis gear to practice for their upcoming match when they were confronted by a group of stern faces. Cathy whispered, "Here's your answer to 'What next in our plans for Independence Day?'"

Mark suspected the crowd approaching the house were birders. They sported trendy outdoor gear: canvas (not leather) hiking boots, pants that can convert to shorts, folding hats, breathable shirts, and cameras and/or binoculars hanging from straps and belts. There were both eager and aggressive elements in their expressions.

Whereas "bird-watchers" like Mark are amateur enthusiasts, birders are list-keeping, species tabulating, habitat studying semi-professionals. He knew the group's back- and/or fanny-packs likely contained water bottles, pocketknives, (waterproof) notebooks, microfiber cleaning cloths, bug spray, flashlight or even headlamp, extra batteries, and medical IDs.

"The leucistic cardinal," said a tall, middle-aged, muscular woman who stepped to the front. "Where is she?" Her hands on her hips—and camera carriers hanging from her belt on each side that resembled holsters—made clear that she expected an immediate and unambiguous answer.

Mark did not respond as she wanted. "Why, he—or she—came to our feeder out back, but we've haven't seen . . . it, them. . . for a few days."

The leader of the group—club? team? pack?—turned to her right, waved the others on, and strode purposefully around the house and toward the garage.

"Uh, excuse us," Cathy said loudly. "I think you might want to ask permission to come onto our property."

"Birds know no boundaries," the lead birder threw over her shoulder without breaking stride. And the group followed her—perhaps bound by some club code of unity or a shared migration instinct.

Cathy pulled on Mark's arm. "Do something!" she pleaded.

He had to race to get in front of them; then he turned and raised his arms. "I'm sorry. You all need to stop where you are. This is not public land accessible to anyone. I think we should return to the street and talk this over." His hands now on his hips, he surveyed the eight faces (he counted them) facing him. Three men, five women with looks of shared purpose.

The spokesperson stepped up almost nose-to-nose with him. "Birds are not private property, Mr. Nelson. And citizens of this great land have the unalienable right to pursue the happiness of looking at, listening to, and—when possible—taking pictures of America's wild birds."

The speech came so easily to her that Mark concluded this wasn't the first time she'd fired both barrels at a non-enthusiast. He stood his ground. "Your right to study birds is not in question here. It's your right to trespass to do so. Now, I'm willing to talk sensibly about this, but not if you insist on this . . . invasion."

Cathy had meanwhile pulled out her cellphone. "This is a very small town, Ma'am. And I need to inform you that the police station—Officer Winston is a friend—is just one block away, the other side of Main Street."

As she spoke, a flock of several dozen geese came honking from farther up the river. They were flying low and then splashed into the river fifty feet from the bulkhead. Mark recalled James Baldwin's reference to male bats honking to females.

The birder spokesperson did not back down. "You have spotted a rare bird, Mr. Nelson, and you cannot reserve this wonder to yourself . . . and your partner." She threw her head in Cathy's direction. Did she mean business partner or some sort of untraditional mate?

Fortunately, one of the other women spoke more softly. "Janice, we can talk out front. I'm sure these nice people will agree to give us a chance to see something so uncommon that we may never have another chance in our lifetimes."

This quieter voice was heeded, and, after some reasoned—and unreasoned—discourse, the Bird Book Club (that was their official name, combining the study of birds in the field and in the literature) agreed to take turns watching in pairs from lawn chairs the Nelson's would provide. Should he or she appear, everyone would have a chance to take pictures.

Mark and Cathy decided to watch discretely from the front hall and the kitchen/family room. She was in back, and he in front for the first shift. Pulling a dining room chair to a living room window, Mark watched and thought.

This group of Americans parked at the head of their driveway was diverse in terms of age, race, and gender. He couldn't speculate about sexual preference. But what they had in common was privilege, whether inherited or earned, assumed or asserted. Their clothes, their equipment, and education revealed their status; and their declaration of their freedom to act endorsed it. How, thought Mark, did we all get to the place in this country where we claimed the right to do pretty much whatever we pleased?

It was probably a generational thing, not of citizens but of citizenship itself. He thought of the neighborhood where he'd grown up in small-town Missouri. Two-bedroom frame and brick houses on small lots in neatly ordered blocks. As the post-war families who lived there raised their baby boomer children, few thought they needed more than what they had.

His father had grown up poor, son of an immigrant craftsman who followed jobs across the Midwest during the Depression. Owning or renting a small house was a benefit of hard work and opportunity. When growth came after the war, Carl bought a small lot close to his brothers and cousins from the old country. And he built perhaps the smallest house his family of three had ever lived in.

It was a simple L-shaped wood structure, with the shorter leg a carpentry shop. It was heated by a wood stove and had only a few stools as furniture (but fine tools, including his one Sears table saw). On his own, he built custom designed furniture for individual clients, and with his two brothers he built solid houses and barns throughout the area.

The longer leg of the L was where he and his wife lived, two rooms plus a bath and a pantry. The living room doubled as bedroom, a Murphy bed that folded away at night into what appeared to a large cabinet by day. They moved their two easy chairs aside when they went to bed. The kitchen was spacious, and that's where they ate. Mark's grandmother kept her cooking supplies—plus canned fruit and vegetables—in a pantry off the kitchen.

Why did Carl and Esther never seek a larger house or attempt to enlarge this one? Simply, he realized what he had was sufficient for their needs.

When his children were grown, Mark's father moved across town to a four-bedroom house with family room beside the kitchen, large patio, and double-car garage—all for two people. Many in the old neighborhoods did the same, turning over their small houses to young families hoping to progress quickly to a residence with children's playroom, storage building for riding mowers and mountain bikes, outdoor plastic gymnasium.

As evidence grew that there would be global shortages of fuel, water, clean air, affordable energy, Americans did not reduce their dreams. Instead, they continued on the foundation of privilege. If an occasional war had to be fought overseas to protect the nation's interests, so be it. There was a class of volunteer military personnel that would take care of these matters for us. We at home would shop.

We would have Disney Land Worlds in every region of the country, sea- and lake-side resorts from coast to coast, luxury cars and big-wheeled trucks to take us where we wanted to go. Our museums and universities would entertain us more than educate us, following a business model based on customer satisfaction. We are entitled to good grades in schools and season passes to all national treasures.

Mark and Cathy were hardly innocent of the benefits of privilege. They lived in a five-bedroom house on a river with modern appliances and all the creature comforts—plus enough money to sustain it. They also had a garage being renovated with a stylish hoist above a loft window and a rediscovered flagpole mounted at one corner. How had it happened? And what could they do about it now?

Reverend James Baldwin aspired to save another mammal species and the souls of his own kind. But he had to be saved by a woman who seldom came to his church and, as far as Mark knew, cared little for bats.

As the changing of the leucistic guard began—two of the party out front marching down the driveway and two more coming back to the front,—Mark muttered to himself, "Save our bats and our birds and our souls,"

"If this group returns," said a voice behind him, causing him to startle, "it will be save yourself, Batman." Cathy had, once again it seemed, read his thoughts.

He hoped, however, that she was just being rhetorical. He worried that he was losing the battle with anxiety. If only he could conceive of an appropriate celebration of their union, perhaps he could keep from obsessing about all the problems still to be resolved before July 4.

Chapter Thirty-One: Enterprise

After a fruitless second day of watching, the Bird Book Club departed, promising/threatening to return. And Cathy announced, "Get ready for a short road trip up past Harbor City. I've found a place to get our patriotic paper plates, napkins, cups, and all the other stuff we need to Bring Forth."

"Good," said Mark, "I've realized we need to get moving on the logistics."

"Party Favorites is one of those beach businesses that caters to vacationers. They buy in bulk and discount everything, especially around holidays."

"So," Mark asked, "swimwear and gear, kites, probably fireworks, too, at this store?"

"Yes," she agreed. "And . . . um . . . novelties."

Cathy got in on the driver's side and propped her phone on the dash so she could follow directions from the GPS. "I found it on the internet, and um, it has a special . . . um . . . section. An extra party favors section for adults only."

"Ah, you mean there are paper products and rubber products in one establishment?"

"I'm not sure what they have, and we don't need to go to that side of the building; but I admit to being a bit curious about the . . . industry."

"Not, I hope, dissatisfied with your love life?"

"Of course not. But all the books on aging say we need to keep learning," she smiled. "Give our interests free rein, so to speak."

The drive from Harbor City to the coast goes from Southern small town to anywhere American beach front in less than an hour. Party Favorites was housed in a corrugated metal dome, with no windows, a giant egg, it seemed to Mark, warming in the mid-summer sun.

What greeted them as they passed through the double-door entrance was a slouching musician at an upright piano crooning "Carolina Moon." Father Time (according to the sign above his head) played and sang as customers walked down crowded aisles inspecting merchandise.

"Well," said Mark. "This is novel." He nodded at the man who wore an Uncle Sam outfit, and the sign for "Novel-T's" over a rack of T-shirts. There were the standards ("My parents went to the beach, and all I got was this lousy T-shirt") and more raunchy ones ("Wet this T-shirt; it'll wet his whistle.") And, of course, all the Carolina Moons were naked rears hanging out of windows.

Cathy elbowed him and turned toward the Independence Day supplies, passing displays of postcards with bathing beauties wearing beauty contest sashes (and nothing else), as well as front and back pictures of musclebound men in thong underwear. Other racks featured standard coffee mugs with the images of fireworks; red, white, and blue flag refrigerator magnets; hats and caps decorated with eagles and canons; and costume paraphernalia (Revolutionary War soldier masks, paper Betsy Ross aprons, pin-on military insignia, and pin-up posters with hip-cocked GI Janes).

"You take this shopping cart," Mark said, pulling one from the rack for Cathy. He arched an eyebrow. "I'll . . . uh . . . buh. . . rowse."

"Buh . . . have," she ordered.

A raspy voice announced over the sound system. "Welcome to OB3X, my friends. Welcome."

"OBX" means the 200 miles of barrier islands stretching from southern Virginia down the cost of North Carolina, a major tourist destination with expanses of open beachfront and the Cape Hatteras National Seashore.

The voice belonged to the piano player, who was now standing beside his instrument—which kept on playing. He patted the upright. "I'm letting Kathy Bates go on auto-pilot, friends, so I can tell you about the great deals we have at OB3X today."

Bates wrote the lyrics to "America the Beautiful," first published as a poem in the July 4, 1895 edition of the church periodical, *The Congregationalist*.

Cathy whispered, "OB3X?"

"Think 'Outer Banks Triple X-rated,'" he whispered back, nodding toward a door in a back corner of the building with the hand-lettered words "Ladies and Gents—Not." Father Time was itemizing the day's deals, though Mark couldn't understand him very well; his speech was jumbled and had an odd rhythm. Then Mark realized he had no teeth and had to gum certain consonants. Through the store's public address system Elvis began crooning slowly, "O beautiful for spacious skies."

Then Time said, winking to Mark, "Hey, friend, I know what you're here for."

Mark looked for a way to put himself at a distance, but he didn't want to head in the direction of "Entertainment for Grown-ups." Father Time's microphone was cordless, though, and he came over beside Mark and put an arm around his shoulder.

"You're hosting the neighborhood block party, I can tell." He held up the microphone and dramatically switched it off. Elvis, picking up the volume, sang that "a thoroughfare for freedom beat . . . Across the wilderness."

"Well . . . ," hesitated Mark.

Time continued, "You just let the missus do her shopping, and I'll make you a good price on all she can fit in a basket— shall we say 25% off?"

He was pulling Mark away from the party goods and toward the "Ladies and Gents—Not" door. Mark tried a diversionary tactic. "I do want to have a look at your fireworks. Do you have . . . um, old-fashioned bottle rockets?"

The choir joined Elvis in singing a "glory-tale / Of liberating strife" and asked that God "refine" America's "gold."

Father Time bragged, "I have bottle rockets, sparky-tail rockets, satellite launchers, foaming Roman rockets, jumbo-stick rockets, and—maybe what you're looking for—Big Boys with Boosters."

Mark slipped his shoulder free of Father Time. "Let me ask you something," he said, turning to face him. "What you have in the room over there is all legal merchandise, I'm sure, but don't you have to spend a lot of time reading regulations, checking tax codes, viewing interstate shipping policies? And liability for your products—especially the fireworks, but also," he nudged the other man's elbow with his elbow, "the, um, toys you have, again, over there. Do you worry about injuries crippling your business?"

Time chuckled as Elvis, speaking softly and not singing, praised the "beautiful for heroes proved / In liberating strife." The orchestra provided a soft background.

"I can tell you're not in the commercial trade, and certainly not an entrepreneur—although," he paused, "you might be looking for tips on how to set up a rival business." He slipped his arm over Mark's shoulder again. "But I'm not worried about competition. You see, this isn't my first rodeo. I learned the ropes setting up similar stores in Nevada, where the trade is less restricted."

"But that wouldn't be the same here," Mark claimed. Now he heard Time's Western twang.

"No, at least not exactly. But if you've been successful somewhere—as I have—you find ways to operate around the rules in other places. In fact, owning your own business in this country is freeing yourself from the constraints that drive others crazy every day."

Elvis looked to a future. "Till all success be nobleness/ And every gain divine." And the choir came in again, as they built toward a rich ending.

Mark nodded, "So, you're able to hide within the grid, avoiding the crosshairs of the system."

"Ah, you're a shrewd one! Yes, I am my own boss with all the rights and privileges that come with the title. Nobody tells me what or what not to do. It's the role the nation's founders imagined for its citizens; but back then they thought of farmers, landowners, not people who buy and sell. But, presto! it's all free enterprise now."

"And time is money," laughed Mark, offering the musician a fist bump. "Thy liberty the law."

Mark again slipped free of Father Time's arm. "Well, I've learned something today. And here comes my purchasing agent." He nodded toward Cathy whose basket was overflowing. "And crown thy good with brotherhood / From sea to shining sea."

"Take this slip with you to check-out, my friend," said Father Time. "It will give her that 25%." He slapped his hand on Mark's back one more time and said loudly, "Y'all come back, now." Then he whispered, "This little catalog will hint at some good things you've missed."

Turning his mic back on, he began singing a song Mark had never heard. "IN--DEE—Pen—Dence." Probably his own composition.

Mark took the pamphlet, tucked inside a brown paper bag, and tucked it in his back pocket. Later he and Cathy would chuckle at the board games (partner swap), lingerie for women and men, XXX-rated (as advertised) digital movies, and brightly colored superhero (with super body parts) comics.

Helping Cathy load the car, Mark glanced back at the clerk, a young woman probably six feet tall, slim, and fit in very short cut-off jeans below a halter-top that revealed a flat belly in front and a round behind in back. "Y'all come back, hear," she had said and slapped Mark on the ass when he walked past.

He had jumped and Cathy had laughed.

As they crossed the parking lot, the sun slipped behind some clouds. Mark asked, "Do I have a sign on my back that says, 'Kick Me'? The old geezer had his hands all over me.

"You do," Cathy chuckled and pulled it off. Then she removed a smaller sign from farther down and held it up so he could read the two lines, "Ameri- / CAN Dream" and see the arrow pointing downward.

The metal building behind them looked more like a bomb than an egg. Mark could hear Father Time bellowing a chorus: "Dancing on the rim of a dime / INN--DEE—pen—dence is sublime."

Chapter Thirty-two: Roots

As he was unloading their purchases from the car, Mark acknowledged with a customary nod his new neighbor Randy (the spouse of his future tennis opponent, Caro-*lyne*) walking absentmindedly down the sidewalk. "Hey," he said.

"Hey," Randy said back and paused at the end of the driveway. "You're from Midwest, my wife told me."

"Yes, small town Missouri. But I've lived most of my adult life in the Old Dominion before retiring here last year." Mark lowered the box labeled "Cones" back into the trunk.

"I thought I could hear your accent when we chatted the other day. I grew up in Arkansas, Pine Bluff, south of Little Rock."

"I see." Mark did not see where this observation might be headed.

Randy asked, "You ever get to know anyone from South Dakota?"

"No, can't say I have, though we took a family vacation in the West and upper Midwest one year, stayed a night in Wall."

"Yeah. Well, I just had a bit of a shock that took me back to childhood . . . well, to high school and a girl I knew from the . . . the Badlands."

Mark thought he looked lost. "Have a seat on the porch here," he gestured to the white wicker chairs arranged around a small table. "I could use a break unloading from the shopping trip of the century. Can I get you a drink, beer?"

"Thanks. Yeah, I'd like that."

When they were settled, Mark asked what had taken him back to his youth, "Something I got in the mail," he said. "If you've time, let me give you the background. You know about small-town life and the nature of 'Fly-over Country.'"

"I do. Midwesterners, they say, have no accent and no culture, so we're overlooked by the big city types on the Coasts— they just pass over or through or around what they think of as empty space. It's not the case that we have no identity. It's just that we tend to be . . . um, understated about ourselves."

Randy chuckled. "That's it."

As they talked, Mak saw that his clothes were more expensive than would be expected in Staffordshire. In fact, he would fit in with the Colony's country club set, perhaps a golfer and a swimmer.

"The fact is," Randy went on, "there are regional differences in the Midwest, too. So, anyway, one day I was working the soda fountain at the Walgreen Drugstore in my hometown, probably mid-1980s, when my co-worker, Jeanne Duncan, bumped into me behind the counter—hip to hip. It caused me to splash milkshake onto the counter in front of a widowed, retired Army colonel at the counter."

"I hope he was spared."

"He was, but I was surprised that this happened because Jeanne and I worked well together, trading workplace duties easily and never crossing the borders between tasks in this tight space. We were like professional—but not romantic— dance partners, turning and sliding, nodding and smiling, bending and gliding."

In his mind Mark substituted Randy's wife Caro-*lyne* for Jeanne and imagined her in Randy's arms, a 1940s Hollywood couple, Fred Astaire and Ginger Rogers.

"But, you know, Jeanne did not acknowledge the collision or offer even a cursory 'I'm sorry.' Of course, L apologized to Colonel Perry, taking a towel to wipe up the spill. He was a regular. Paying special attention to him sometimes produced a tip."

"Tips weren't as customary back then as they are now," offered Mark. "You learn to spot those customers likely to appreciate extra effort."

"Correct. He brushed it off with a wave of his hand. I smiled my relief and saw him smile at what Jeanne did next, which was to lean close to a young man sitting on the short leg of the counter, either to ask him something or to listen to something he had to say."

Mark took a sip of his beer. "Is it possible you had special interest in Jeanne?"

"It is. But right then I was an innocent 15-year-old, and this hip bump—completely unconscious on Jeanne's part—becomes an important event in a painfully slow adolescent discovery of the physical aspect of romance."

Mark laughed. "I thought mine was the last innocent generation! Of course, you, too, were without the education the internet now provides our children."

"Oh, I may have been an exception. But what I got in the mail today turns Jeanne's hip jolt into a landmark in my confrontation with death as well as sex."

Mark felt a jolt at a casual conversation about teenage attraction jumping to the end of life.

Randy went on. "When the rush had slowed and we were washing dishes together at the soda fountain's double sink, I asked, 'What was that?' Jeanne turned toward me with a friendly smile and asked, 'What was what?'"

"Ouch. I've been there, too--interpreting a casual encounter for more than it was."

"Yes, it hurt.. Now, Jeanne's and my teamwork had been achieved in part because she was five years older than I was, which meant there was never any electricity between us. She knew how to dance around a boy and how to dance up to a man. I was no more masculine to her than a refrigerator."

"Ouch, again. I get it." Mark knew Randy would assume they talking about universal male adolescent experiences. But he was also recalling the closeness with Randy's wife in the back of their boutique store-to-be, her shoulder bumping his.

Randy explained, "Jeanne's matter-of-fact response is simply a sign of her greater experience. I, however, at fifteen would jump at any girl's touch as if it was the initiation of profound intimacy. Now, here's the funny thing about all this: the word root."

Mark raises his eyebrows. Surely, he's not talking about the male organ?

"The distance between my innocence and Jeanne's sophistication is underscored by her upper Midwestern pronunciation of a few words, one especially common in soda fountain jargon: 'root beer.' Everyone I know had always said the first word to rhyme with 'boot'; but Jeanne pronounced it to rhyme with 'put.' That must be how they say it in South Dakota."

"Odd," agrees Mark. He tried it out: "Boot and root; put and root. Root beer."

Randy nods. "Today's mail takes me to another meaning in the beer" half of that soft drink's name. That's where I'm heading. Farewell, Robert Duncan."

Mark did not follow. "Who is Robert Duncan."

"He was the customer Jeanne went over to talk with at the other part of the counter. I demanded to know why she hadn't noticed her collision with a friend, me, but was chummy with someone I thought was a stranger."

"But she did know him?"

"Oh, yes. Jeanne said to me, 'Oh, you mean that very attractive young man at the end of the counter?' And I said yes. And I remember to this day how she laughed and squeezed my arm. 'That was my husband. He's in the Army and stationed at Pine Bluff. That's why I'm here.'"

"Ah," said Mark. "She'd come down from South Dakota to be close." Pine Bluff Arsenal was one of the places that manufactured Agent Orange, the defoliant used to clear jungle in Vietnam.

Randy went on. "It had never occurred to me to ask about her life away from the drug store. But she and Robert were both from Fargo, both from military families. I came from a working-class family, and my parents cheered at the end of the draft. She and I came, that is to say, from different roots (roots rhyming with "boots," not "foots" or "spouts")."

Mark put things together. "And today you read something about Jeanne."

"That's right." He took out his phone and read: 'Another casualty in America's longest war. Sergeant First Class Robert Duncan, of Fargo, South Dakota, was killed in a bomb attack in Iraq. He leaves behind a wife, Jeanne, two children, three grandchildren.'"

"That's sad," Mark said. "I'm afraid civilians these days don't pay much attention to the cost of the country's commitments to, as they call it, 'foster democracy abroad.'"

Randy sighed. "That's how the other part of 'root beer' was redefined for me: a bier is a stand on which a coffin is placed."

Chapter Thirty-three: Tarps

Mark came back from buying red, white, and blue clotheslines and citronella candles at the hardware store to hear Beverly telling Cathy that she was having trouble finding enough canopies. The plan had been to put them over tables the Methodist church was loaning them.

"Apparently, there's another party in town, and those folks made arrangements to get them from Sal's Junk Shop." Sal sold goods on consignment, but had, over the years, acquired a stockpile of miscellaneous items available for rent.

Mark rubbed his chin. "I thought you'd talked to Sal at the store two weeks ago."

"I did, and I didn't think there'd be any problem. She didn't ask for a deposit."

"Is the other party on the 4th also?" asked Cathy.

"The day before."

"Mark and I can go out there this afternoon. Maybe we can work out a deal with the other party hosts to get the canopies from them early on the morning of Independence Day. It would save them carting them to Sal. And she wouldn't have to do anything except collect money."

"That might work. But be careful with her," advised Beverly. "She's a shrewd dealer, and if she gives you something, she'll ask for something in return."

"Okay. I'll let you know. If this doesn't work, we'll need a plan C."

Not wanting to leave this key part of the plan in limbo, Cathy insisted they drive out Wharf Street after lunch. On the way Mark brought up a question that had occurred to him, "I don't mean to stereotype. And it wouldn't matter, but I was wondering if you thought Sal might be Jewish."

The junk shop proprietor did speak with an accent—or in a manner that didn't conform to the sounds and rhythms of eastern North Carolina. Mark was reluctant to ask where she was from, and he could find no one knew her last name. Signs in the business and on her card simply said, "Sal."

"Hmm," mused Cathy. "Hadn't thought about it. Physical features don't contradict it, but, you're right, we don't want to classify business owners as likely from one race. You, after all, are—or were—a bank employee."

There was plenty of open parking at the Junk Shop ("Home of Good Goods"), as it was the last business to stay afloat in the doomed Olde Towne Shopping Center. The Center, perhaps a football field and a half long, was less than a mile from downtown. It was bordered on the west by railroad tracks, on the east by a plant nursery. There was a hundred or more feet of land too soggy to build on the north side down to the river. Across the street was the Senior Center, the (one-room) public library, tennis and basketball courts.

The investors in the shopping center had, like most other Americans, failed to see the 2008 recession coming. At one time there had been a generic shoe store, a Dollar Market, and a barber shop in the strip mall that went from south to north. A fried chicken drive-through stood alone beside Wharf Street, and it stayed in business until the family running it lost the will to work twelve hours a day six days a week.

The area was in between mostly white homes (east) and mostly black homes (west), with some mixed blocks on both sides. All the downtown stores (a single block) were owned by whites, and their political power put obstacles in the path of potential rivals. Some residents spoke of a revitalization plan that would expand support to Olde Towne; but, with the original investors having pulled out, funding was now the challenge.

Cathy and Mark found Sal sitting at a large mahogany desk behind a glass display case. A heavyset, middle-aged woman with the hint of a mustache, she wore a dress shirt with no tie and dark brown khaki slacks. An old phonograph was on a smaller table behind her, and she had a stack of vinyl records from the 1960s: Aretha Franklin, the Rolling Stones, Jimi Hendrix. She had three loaded on the machine, and the Beatles' *Sgt. Peppers Lonely Hearts Band* was coming out from behind armoires, under L-shaped sofas, inside kitchen cabinets.

On a library table next to the desk were a xerox machine, a fax, and an old library card catalog cabinet where she kept her inventory lists. Sal rang up sales on an old hand crank cash register and made out receipts by hand.

She greeted the Nelsons with a wide smile. "Ah, the party hosts. I understand you might need some supplies for the event. Come this way, please."

Furniture, display cases, and bins full of books, magazines, and DVDs created a maze through which Sal navigated smoothly. She stepped around a tall dresser, went between two grandfather clocks (one possibly an antique, the other more modern), and circled a massive pump organ. Mark and

Cathy followed in single file, as there was no extra room along her path. Cathy whispered over her shoulder, "How does she know why we're here?"

"Hmph," Mark replied softly. "Everyone else in Staffordshire knows, as does Father Time in the next county!"

He stubbed his toe on a vacuum clearer poking out beside a giant chifforobe. He smothered an "ouch" and limped—inconspicuously, he hoped—to catch up with Cathy. Walking in the Junk Shop was like dodging cypress knees and soggy spots in his lower yard. He recalled He Who Travels Well telling him he shouldn't see the knees as obstacles in his way, but as landmarks to recognize and rely on. Apparently, Sal operated in the correct way in her store.

She continued her winding journey around an assortment of old garden tools and through a door to a fenced-in area out back where there was an array of picnic tables faded by the sun, plastic outdoor furniture, lawn umbrellas, tents, and canopies wrapped around their support poles. "Now," she said, "these are the ones I *can't* let you rent."

"Can't?" asked Cathy. "So, why are you showing us?"

"Ma'am, that is the question. I want you to know what I had to offer two weeks back, so you'll know I carry generally good merchandise. Over here," now waved a hand, "are some, um, less elegant options."

She pulled back a movable wood and canvas screen to reveal several dozen suitcase-sized bags. "In each of these," she explained, "is a twelve-foot by twelve-foot tarp. I've got garden bean poles you can use to set them up over your tables—make your own canopies."

Cathy leaned over to open the case and saw faded military surplus camouflage material. "'Less elegant, yes," she said.

"And putting them up so they're not going to blow down or away wouldn't be easy."

Sal noted, "Beverly is good at this sort of thing. So, is Raymond Winston, by the way, when he's sober. Putting these up—designed and used by our Marines in the Middle East—would be a patriotic statement for Independence Day, one that your guests would appreciate."

Mark asked, "Are the poles strong enough?" He hefted one case. "These are heavier than the butter beans you would have hanging from strings."

"They'll do. And you can wrap them in red, white, and blue crape to contribute to the overall effect. I have some in stock."

Mark looked at Cathy. She shrugged slightly. "We'd do best to put a deposit down."

On the circuitous way back to the front, Cathy tugged on Mark's arm and pulled him toward a set of shelves. They were full of North Carolina lighthouse models, each distinctive but still forming a collection of similar shapes and colors. There were replicas of lighthouses at Albemarle Sound, Cape Hatteras, Ocracoke, Wilmington, and Cape Fear.

"Which of these is not like the others?" she giggled, echoing a question asked of kids watching *Sesame Street* in the 1970s that was designed to teach them similarity and difference.

Mark recognized the allusion but didn't see the answer at first. Then he noticed a Montauk, New York, lighthouse on a tall thin bookcase behind the shelves. "What's that doing here, I wonder?"

Sal, who had come up beside them, explained, "That's

the first American landmark that generations of immigrants saw when they sailed into New York. To many, it's as much a symbol of a new home as the Statue of Liberty."

"Interesting," said Mark. "But does it have anything written on it as memorable as 'Give me your tired, your poor, / Your huddled masses yearning to breathe free'?"

Sal huffed. "Trust me, it sends the message."

Sal wasn't exactly pushing them away from the lighthouses, but she could have been crowding them toward the front. She brightened. "And you might be interested to know the man who designed it is also responsible for the Cape Henry Lighthouse in Virginia."

Mark said, "We've seen that. It marks the southern entrance to the Chesapeake Bay. Patrick Henry lived there, as I remember. It's where, they say, he composed his 'Liberty or Death' speech."

"I kind of like the Montauk lighthouse," said Cathy, looking back at it. "I didn't see a price tag on it."

Again, Sal's tone darkened. "It's not for sale." She waved them toward the cash register. "Listen: I don't really need a deposit on the tarps. It's not likely anyone else will want them. Just let me know a few days before if you plan to use them."

When they were in the car, Cathy said, "Well, we have a back-up plan. But that business of the New York lighthouse was a bit strange."

Mark agreed. "It must matter to her personally. But, if so, why was it out on the floor?"

As they drove home, Mark thought: "Now I know what to arrange for our anniversary."

Chapter Thirty-four: Matches

Mark and Cathy did not lose or win their match with Caro-lyne! Lee and her partner (who did turn out to be Les Moore). The game was called when Dusty Sherman made an emergency landing in the parking area of Old Towne Center just across the street from the courts.

Before that dramatic event, as they were getting their rackets and balls out ahead of the match, Mark asked Caro-lyne how the store was coming along. She shrugged. "I fear we may have to change our emphasis somewhat. This conservative community seems to observe conservative values in terms of . . . substance consumption."

He laughed. "It's more that the area is traditional—alcohol is the drug of choice, has been for as long as there've been white folks."

"Randy also seems to have cooled on the original idea. He thinks there are more clientele who will appreciate fine beer and wine, imported and domestic."

"If I were evaluating a business—not exactly in my former role as a public relations officer, but more as a local—I would say that market is not crowded."

Les, the chiropractor with no office and no overhead who didn't take insurance, smiled. "It's an open field, to be sure."

They stood, stretched, and went on the court to warm up.

Cathy and Mark realized quickly they were outclassed. Cathy at ten years younger would have been a match for Ca-ro-*lyne*, but Mark could see her partner had been holding back when they'd played a few weeks ago.

As they practiced, he watched his opponent's easy movement and sound strokes. Seeing how easily he found the right place to put the ball (and then did so), Mark concluded he'd violated an unspoken rules of social interaction. For a friendly game among neighbors, he should have confessed his skills and experience.

Mark had always loved tennis because of its fixed boundaries and rules. Balls were in (even when on the line) or out (wide or long). If a racket hit the net, it cost the player points. A foot stepping over the baseline line meant a fault.

But within those confines there was enormous flexibility. Players with good ground strokes could stay behind the baseline and wear down their opponents by scattering shots from side to side, eventually exploiting a weak backhand or forehand.

Others with quick reflexes and good eyes could come to the net and cut off even hard hit balls, angling them out of their opponent's reach. The best of those players could bend low to pick off balls at mid-court before closing in to dominate the net. They had to be prepared to backpedal and handle a lob, but they learned to detect the kind of backswing that meant it was coming.

In other words, there was, Mark believed, freedom in a fixed system. It was true in most other human endeavors, his own profession, for instance. Respect the truth and your audience, he reminded himself daily. And he told his junior colleagues, if you recognize appropriate boundaries and work within them, you will be successful.

When the two couples changed sides, down five games to none, he whispered to Cathy. "I guess we'll play for the enjoyment of the game."

She admitted. "We don't have much choice. But they are

fun to watch."

Caro-*lyne* was fun to watch, thought Mark. Her tight outfit was perfect for her slim, muscular figure.

Tossing the ball over his head to serve a minute later, Mark spotted an airplane flying low across town and toward the tennis courts. The engine sound increased dramatically as the plane raced above them

"Is he in trouble?" asked Caro-*lyne*, one hand shading her eyes against the sun.

They could hear the engine sputter and see the plane bank left and right as it went across Wharf Street and over Sal's Junk Shop.

"That's Dusty," said Mark. Seeing blank looks on the faces of Les and Caro-*lyne*, he explained. "You've seen him, spraying crops. The bright orange biplane. He's doing everyone's corn this time of year."

Dusty was a familiar sight to most residents, as he flew low; and his plane was distinctive. He was like a fighter bomber in World War II movies, zooming down to spray enemy positions, then pulling up and banking sharply to evade anti-craft fire. Some said Dusty had been part of an Air Force flight demonstration squadron, something like the Blue Angels.

The plane went out over the river, gaining a bit of altitude. But then small puffs of smoke trailed behind, and he swung around to come at them again.

"He's going to land in the river or on top of us," said Caro-*lyne*.

And it seemed she was right, as *Buff* began dropping and then climbing up as it approached. Then the engine went out, the propeller slowing to the point it was visible as separate blades and not a blur.

It didn't come down in the river, however, but rose over the bank, leveled out for a bit, and then banged down at the far end of the parking area. The wheels squealed as they caught the pavement, and the plane bounced up into the air and down to the concrete several times as it raced toward Wharf Street. Fortunately, there were no vehicles in its way.

Mark tried to calculate the direction the plane would travel—if the pilot could keep it going straight—and decide whether to race left or right. Cathy pulled him toward the library. "This way," she insisted.

Caro-*lyne* and Les, farther away from the street and the plane, seemed frozen on the other side of the net.

With a final screech and a few more hops, Buff crossed the sidewalk and stopped in the middle of Wharf Street, the propellers just touching the high fence that surrounded the tennis courts.

There were now no flames or smoke coming from the engine. The pilot lifted the cockpit top, hinged at the back, from the inside and propped it open behind him. His goggles were loose around his neck, and he pulled his gloves free of his hands. "I hope I didn't disturb your game," Dusty smiled.

As he climbed backwards down the ladder from the cockpit Cathy realized why he'd named his plane *Buff*. He clearly worked out himself. Rounded shapes were taut in his aviator pants and flight jacket.

"How you doing, Dusty?" asked a voice from the other side of the plane, someone Mark and Cathy couldn't see.

"Good. You, Sal?"

The junk shop owner came around the tail of the plane, looking down its length as if she were an FAA inspector. "Glad you didn't come into the shop," she said. "I've got good sales on glass items, and I think you would have been like the proverbial bull."

He chuckled. "Like everyone else in Staffordshire, I know the importance of your store. I'd have put *Buff* in the drink if I thought it might cause damage to a local institution."

Seeing Mark and Cathy, Sal responded, "These folks were about to buy a lighthouse sculpture, another fragile item I wouldn't want you crashing into."

"I was not in free fall," he insisted. "*Buff* had just become a glider. I was coasting in without power, but the controls kept me in a proper alignment—you know, flaps up to stay up and then down to slow the plane, keep it from pulling left or right. Pretty smooth, after all."

"Uh-hum."

Caro-*lyne* had come up to the fence to join Mark and Cathy. "Were you scared up there, Mr. Pilot?" she asked in a child's voice and with a hand on her throat.

He chuckled. "It's Dusty, Miss. Dusty Sherman. And, no, things were pretty much under control, though . . ." He looked at the plane. "I could use some help getting *Buff* out of the road. Don't want to get a traffic ticket. The five of us should be able to do it."

Five? thought Mark. He counted Dusty, Sal, and three tennis players. Les Monroe had disappeared. He also wondered where the Staffordshire police were. Had no one reported this?

But Dusty was right. Directing them to different positions,

he was able to maneuver the plane so the wheels went over the entrance to the parking lot not the curb, and together they got it into the lot.

"I assume you won't take off back the way you came," said Mark. "Once you . . . what? fix the engine."

Dusty laughed. "No. We've got a trailer we can load the plane onto and take it back to the field. I don't see any structural damage."

Her eyes sweeping up and down Dusty's structure, Ca-ro-*lyne*! proposed, "Why don't we all go to . . . um, somewhere . . . to file an after-action report or whatever?"

"Your place or mine?" the pilot grinned.

Chapter Thirty-five: Dizziness

Saturday night Mark woke up Cathy by staggering into the dresser, rattling her jewelry case, and throwing an arm into the venetian blinds on the bedroom window. He meant to be taking one of those routine trips inspired by his enlarged prostate ("half again as big as a walnut," his doctor had said). He'd started toward the bathroom, found himself veering strongly to the left, and reached out for any kind of support.

He fell back into the bed, which was spinning counterclockwise. Cathy told him to move to the recliner—slowly "I think this has to do with your inner ear."

"My ear, the hell! It's my entire head, where crop-dusters are circling beekeepers, bears are setting off fireworks, toothless porn dealers are avoiding arrest by our underwater surveillance squad who've come ashore for purposes of national security."

His spinning out words encouraged her to think he wasn't that bad off. "You're anticipating disaster in Bring Fourth, but it's going to be fine. We have all the paper goods, Beverly has arranged for tables, chairs, and even canopies."

"Ha! She wants to launch pigeons from the garage loft door just to make me dizzy. As they orbit around my broken head, I'll stumble on cypress knees, fall into a sink hole, and disappear like the Prohibition era boozers of Staffordshire."

"Your inner ear is where balance is controlled. Something's out of whack in there, and lying flat can make it worse, so we need to see how you do upright—but not standing upright yet!

"I'm hardly an upright citizen, but let me see what I can do."

He made it to the chair, but the room was still spinning. She held his hand, and they waited together. As she predicted, the dizziness subsided, and she began to think maybe it was a panic attack. Of course, there was also aging to consider.

In the morning, however, she thought it would be good for him to see an ear, nose, and throat specialist. Under her intense questioning, Mark admitted he'd had previous spells, though not as severe. To himself, he admitted that the increasing complications to July 4 were more and more troublesome. He feared Cathy was becoming so irritated with him that she would demand marital counseling . . . or worse.

Cathy searched the internet and found an ENT doctor in Harbor City. When she explained the suddenness and severity of the attack, his receptionist told them to come at the lunch hour. She would squeeze them in.

The diagnosis came quickly. "This is likely positional vertigo; it's not uncommon," Dr. Wheeler explained. "These particles, crystals, suspended inside your ear help you keep your balance; but they can get out of alignment. If they migrate to the wrong place, you can't sense up from down. You're lucky you didn't go head-over-heels down the stairs."

To confirm his diagnosis the doctor had Mark sit on the examining table, took him by the shoulders, and pushed him over on his side. After five seconds, he pulled him to a sitting position. Then, after another brief pause, he shoved him the other way. Mark thought he might throw up.

"See? I'm throwing those crystals around in there. Makes you dizzy."

"Yeah! But what do I do?" he asked. The poster-sized diagram of a giant eye on the wall in front of him was rotating counterclockwise. (He would later conclude that it was a personal insult that there was an eye but not an ear decorating this examination room.)

Dr. Wheeler smiled, "There's a simple, cost-free treatment."

"'Cost-free'? That alone is almost enough to sober me up."

He explained the Brandt-Daroff exercise, which involves throwing one's torso and head back and forth, just as he had done, three times a day. If Mark performed this maneuver faithfully at home, pausing for five seconds in each position, he would be over the vertigo in a few days. He should continue the routine, however, for a week to ten days.

Riding back to Staffordshire, Mark asked, "No canceling of the celebration, then?"

"Not a chance. Think, in fact, of where we are in the whole process: invitations out and getting good response; people letting us know how many guests they're bringing—as well as offering to help. I've made a list of families and the dishes they're contributing."

"It sounds good—on paper," he grumped.

"Big Bob is dropping off the grill the night before. Beverly is set to deliver the burgers and fries, Fireworks Tom is eager to entertain—at a safe distance. Oh, and tables and chairs from the Methodists, half a dozen volunteers bringing coolers with soft drinks."

"Weather permitting," he grumped.

"It's always hot on July 4, but we'll get shade from the house and trees by the afternoon. And there's almost always a river breeze; plus, we have two large circular fans brought down from attics as back-ups."

"However, they'll meet hot air from a number of the guests," he grumped.

"You've drawn a diagram of where tables and chairs can go in the yard with the grill in the garage doorway. I love the little American flags beside cypress knees to mark a path in the lower yard down to the dock. Another sketch specifies how salads go on the picnic table (under netting that will keep out flies); cakes, cookies, and brownies on the kitchen island; pies and shortcakes on the kitchen table. Finally, drinks are in coolers along the garden in the side yard."

"We won't have enough trash cans," he grumped.

"Beverly has found twenty collapsible, plastic garbage containers that, folded, fit in the garage. Some are labeled 'Recycle' and others 'Dump.' Boy and Girl Scout families have volunteered to be a clean-up crew.

"What could go wrong?" he grumped.

They pulled into their driveway and went into the family room. "I'm going to do this exercise right now on the sofa," he said, plumping down in the middle and pushing cushions aside. "Then I'll make a chart to keep track of when I do it for the next few days."

"And I'll be your coach, making sure you don't cut corners. I've got just the thing for record keeping." She pulled a calendar from the junk drawer at the kitchen counter and turned it so he could see the cover picture—a bikini-clad female aerial acrobat poised on a trapeze."

"Where'd you get that? Not that it's not inspiring."

"Father Time slipped into our basket. Each month has a different theme and a different cover girl—or boy." She opened it to July and showed Mark a rear view of a naked Olympic javelin contestant at the end of his throw."

He chuckled. "I'm not doing my Brandt-Daroff in my birthday suit."

"I may change your mind about that. But now, about the party—there is, um, one thing," said Cathy tentatively. She was holding one of the fresh apples they'd bought, turning it around in one hand.

"Here it comes!" He was bent over on his left side, the dizziness there but not overwhelming.

'It's not bad. It's good, in fact." Cathy gestured for him to resume the exercise by sitting up. She turned around to wash the apple in the sink. "We've been invited to that other party on the 3rd. Charlene is involved. And she reached out to us and some others in our . . . set."

"Argh! One more thing to worry about. Afternoon, casual, celebratory? At her house?"

"The time is that afternoon, but location is a spot upriver.

We've driven by the turnoff many times. It's been organized by a group of black churches in the area, led by the American Methodist Episcopal Church, as a kind of a belated Juneteenth event."

"The end of slavery. Well, I guess I can get behind that." He threw himself over on his right side, beginning to feel the vertigo a bit more strongly.

"Good. Now, it may be a little more . . . um, joyous than you Midwesterners are comfortable with. You know, singing and dancing, group things." She took a bite of her apple, held it out and examined it. "Want one?"

"In a bit," he said. "Maybe they'll play 'Hey, Jude' just for me."

"Or, well, there could be some . . . rap or certainly soul music."

"Um-hm." He brought himself upright. The room was less stable.

"And we should be prepared to participate in a game of horseshoes or softball."

"Good grief! Well, no stealing bases for us, and right field is the place to be. All the action goes to left."

Cathy gestured for him to throw himself the other way, to his left. "Now, I'm not sure why, but Charlene has asked if you'll say a prayer. You know, before the meal."

He felt his world spinning again.

"We'll have a grand time twice over this year," she smiled. Then she sang, "Lift ev'ry voice and sing, / Til earth and heaven ring, / Ring with the harmonies of Liberty."

He thought to himself that positional vertigo might not be such a bad thing, if properly timed

Chapter Thirty-six: Behind

"My backside," Mark said, gesturing, "is in these pants."

Cathy looked up from her iPad but said nothing.

He continued. "At an earlier stage of our marriage, I wouldn't have been so direct. I might have said, 'I left it upstairs in a dresser drawer.' Or 'I decided not to wear it tonight.' That still would have directed your attention to the subject. But the many years we've been together allow me now to speak directly."

She frowned, not looking up. She turned a page on her iPad, sweeping her finger across the screen. A central feature of her retirement was reading novels, both literary and popular.

"Of course," added Mark, "the rest of my equipment is in there, too. I thought I'd start from the back and work forward, though. Make it seem more like progress than just itemizing."

He stood with his back to her now, gazing out the family room windows as the afternoon winds stirred up the river. Might be a storm, he thought.

Cathy asked, "Are you having another panic attack about the party?"

It was only two days away, and he was concerned about a tropical storm coming up the coast of Georgia. He had also received a threatening note from the Bird Book Club about their "freedom" to set up a leucistic cardinal watch on what they were calling "Independents" Day.

He turned again to face her. "Have I ever told you about Mr. Clean?"

"The man on the cleaner bottle? Let's say that you have." She turned back to her iPad. "Plus, you told me that Douglas, the Whole Donut Man, looked like him."

"That's true. But there was also a man in my neighborhood growing up who resembled the drawing Ernie Allen created for the popular cleanser."

"I know the figure. Bald head, pale eyebrows, big smile. Always with his arms crossed in front of the white T-shirt. An American advertisement icon."

"Right. Now, the guy in my hometown, a dentist, was different from the Donut Guy, who has scars on his arms, his neck, his face—presumably from burns that come with his profession."

"You told me Fireworks Tom has the same thing. So?

"I'm thinking about the scars we hide from each other. We keep them, so to speak, under wraps. But these guys don't. And Mr. Clean of my youth must not have. "

"You're shifting from physical scars to emotional scars, I think. Are things coming up from your past that have marked you? Like Bruce, your fellow correspondent, being killed in Vietnam?"

"I guess I am. We all have these experiences we cover over in the same way our clothes cover our . . . well, our asses. But then something rips the mask away and the scars are exposed."

"You're beginning to scare me. Is it more than the party that's worrying you?"

"It's not that serious—I hope. But something happened at the grocery store the other day that made me realize society keeps things covered just as we conceal our personal injuries."

"Go on."

"Okay. Let me back up to what happened one Saturday morning in the drug store where I worked as a naive teenager, an uncovering, so to speak. By the way, it was interesting that Randy Lee had the same job when he was growing up that I did. Anyway, this story will lead me back to the food store in Staffordshire."

"Uh-oh. Did the dentist drop his pants on you? Or did he want you to drop yours?"

"No, not exactly. But the man—I'm sorry I don't remember his name—wore outfits that revealed giant pecs, a neck become more shoulders, forearms bulging from the short sleeves of his white T-shirt. And, I need to mention, he had no scars. I wonder now, in fact, whether he shaved his arms to make them 'clean.'"

She asked, "Was Mr. Clean not only lean but tall also?"

"Yes. I'd guess about six three, which was large for that time. He didn't smile as much as the real Mr. Clean. Hmm, the 'real Mr. Clean.' That doesn't quite make sense, but you know what I mean. Our Mr. Clean was a real person, but also, it seemed to me, an imitation of something not real."

"Was he truly bald, or did he shave his head?"

"He might have. Clearly, he wanted to create a persona, be a recognizable figure."

"Ahead of the times, though. Didn't Schwarzenegger come later?"

"Yes, although there were famous bodybuilders in the

movies then—Steve Reeves, for instance. But let's just conclude for now that our Mr. Clean stood out in a small town; there was no one who looked like him."

"Okay, his body was his trademark." She chuckled again. "I can imagine his dentist's business card. 'Washboard Abs Scrub Your Smile Clean.'"

"Hmm. Well, I worked as a soda jerk at Bunns' Drug Store on Main Street, popular lunch spot for the downtown business and professional crowd."

He heard distant thunder and turned to look at the darkening skies over the river.

"Did you get your butt pinched by secretaries and sales ladies as you went to and fro?"

He frowned. "That didn't happen. But here's the thing: Mr. Clean did kind of goose me."

"Ah, he knew your behind was in your pants!"

"He must have. Now, what brought this moment to mind is two things: first, the number of naked men we've seen on television lately."

Binge watching filled their evenings as Bring Fourth filled their days. They started with the cocktail hour at 6:00, watched an episode, fixed dinner, watched another before bed.

"They have left little to the imagination, male or female," Cathy agreed.

"It was only in 1973, you know, that Radar, in *M*A*S*H* showed his bare behind on network television—a shocker at the time. Mainstream movies—at least the American versions—were even more discrete. So, what has brought this anatomical feature literally out in the open?"

"I think you're going to tell me." She grinned and tilted her head to one side. "And maybe even show me."

"On that," he laughed, "We'll see. Okay, Mr. Clean came up to the cash register at the same time as Miss Tompkins, 10th grade English teacher. I was behind the counter, but I spotted a spill, some liquid, on the floor right in front of her—a beautiful woman, by the way, a major object of fantasy. I grabbed a towel off the counter and squatted to wipe it up."

"And there was your plumber's butt?"

"I assume so. Anyway, Mr. Clean did two things: 1) he said, 'Get up, son, don't be teasing this young lady that way.' And 2) he put the toe of one shoe under me and kind of lifted."

"Hmm."

"It wasn't a kick, just an upward pressure right on . . . um, the bottom of my bottom."

"Hmm."

"It was puzzling at the time, but now it seems more suggestive because we know so much more about sex acts, about . . . um . . . various desires."

Cathy agreed. "Many things were hidden from us when we were children. More from girls than boys, I'm sure."

"Agreed. Now, here's another thing: I had no idea back then what might tease a teacher, but I certainly didn't think it would be a glimpse of my backside. I thought that maybe it was just that I was trying to please her, to move a mess out of her way. And she would appreciate that—no falling down, you see."

"Ah, but as you've explained, men's backsides are now seen in new ways by the current generation. And those teenage boys who let their pants fall down their butts probably know something about that."

"So, a question is: how many of our scars can we bear to bare, so to speak? And do we even know what the scars are or what confrontation of them will do to us?"

"I'm glad you didn't go into the 'Ladies and Gents—Not' room at Party Favorites! But I'm going to insist that you resist too much introspection ahead of the party. I'll need you dressed and healed for the event."

Her iPad dinged at the same time the (repaired) doorbell rang, and she glanced at the screen. "Hmm," she said. "Front door. But, assuming there's more, you can finish this tale later."

Chapter Thirty-seven: Baggage

It was Beverly at the door with, she announced, "good news and bad news."

"Come in out of the weather," said Cathy. "And give us the bad news first."

They walked back to the family room. As they passed the stairway in the hall they could hear the rain falling on the tin roof two floors up. Mark worried, "I hope this is short-lived. I don't want our yard any wetter than it already is when Big Bob shows up with his grill and tables, chairs, and . . . the canopies of some sort arrive."

"The weather is not going to be a problem," Beverly assured him. "All the forecasts say it will stop early in the evening and dry out before the guests arrive Sunday. The bad news is that—well, it's not really bad news. The Juneteenth folk are happy to let you use Sally's canopies. In fact, they're going to pack them up and bring them here about 4:00 on the Fourth."

"Why is that a problem?" wondered Mark. "Our party starts at 5:00."

Cathy answered him. "They're going to look like hired workers on Water Street—you know, as in many social events around here for many years. Blacks from one area of town serving whites in another."

"Ah," signed Mark. "Couldn't we persuade them to let us come over there?"

Beverly shrugged, "It's their decision."

Cathy said, "There is an easy solution: we invite them to stay for a bit at the party, enjoy the food and drink and some socializing. We'll be at their event; they come here."

"Whoa! We would need to get more of everything!" fussed Mark. "The others aren't bringing doubles dishes."

"I bet the folks at the Juneteenth event will have leftover dishes. Folks aways do."

Mark still resisted. "We need more help setting up for how many . . . ? An extra fifteen, twenty?"

Beverly shrugged. "It won't be that bad. I've been getting offers of help from lots of folks, even have a list. I'll get them to be here around 3:00 before the canopies arrive. And . . . well, I don't want to give too much away, but you're going to have more help than you think."

Cathy added a concern of her own. "Are you sure about this? I'm guessing there have not been too many . . . um . . . mixed social events outside of school sponsored ones."

Beverly agreed. "Yes, some Water Street folk will be a bit surprised, especially as this is a neighborhood event and extra guests won't have been announced. Still, the time could be right. I think that's what Charlene thinks, inviting you over there in the first place."

Mark could see the sky lighting up and the wind dying down. He also concluded that the two women had, as usual, decided this issue. "So, the general idea stays the same; we just increase the number involved. I'd better study my plans," He opened his notebook on the kitchen island.

Beverly and Cathy sat down at the table in front of the bay windows and began to review the list of food and drinks they were providing. Guests were to bring any alcoholic drinks they wanted; and, of course, each family would have one or more dishes to contribute to the feast. It was not quite the loaves of bread and the fish with which Jesus' disciples fed the multitude, but they believed there would be plenty.

Glancing at Mark, engrossed in his plans, Beverly leaned close to tell Cathy. "You remember that I'm a lawyer, right?"

Cathy nodded, raising her eyebrows.

"Well, I've actually been doing double duty in Stafford-shire this summer—handy-womanizing, yes, but also doing background work on property sales in the area. I'm identifying the little people—like you and me—but also the wheelers and dealers, the ones who seem to be moving toward some larger goal outside of home building and land ownership."

"Mark and I are here to enjoy retirement, not launch new careers."

"Of course. There are only a handful of big wigs amassing land in town and in the county. They're the ones we want to identify and watch."

"Hmm. Charlene alluded to possible schemes related to the replacement of the Short Bridge. Is that your main focus?"

"That's one piece of the puzzle, to be sure. There's potential in Staffordshire for development of the good and the bad kind. We don't want to become a resort community of condominiums, vacation cabins, chain motels, and restaurants."

"And you're telling me this now because . . . ?"

"Well, among other reasons, we think you should keep your ears open and your eyes wide during this holiday event. Use the party to draw people out, see what you can learn. Okay?"

Cathy said that she would. And Beverly assured her they would talk more of this later. She recommended that she explain it all to Mark at the right time.

Right now was not the right time, Cathy knew. Her husband was obsessing about the next two days. And there may have been something else hinted at in his story of Mr. Clean. As they were getting ready for bed, she asked him about the day he was goosed by a dentist. "It has stayed in your memory—why?"

"Well, I think the figure of the Whole Donut Man brought it up a few weeks ago. Then, the other day, when I was getting groceries, one of the female checkers revealed her behind in almost the same way I did long ago. She'd noticed a candy bar—a Mounds, I believe—that had rolled under the gum rack opposite her register."

"And she was wearing low-cut jeans. Maybe just a thong. Did she turn her back to you, give you a view?"

"Well, she did, but I don't know if that was deliberate or an accident."

"Was she, by any chance, a muscular woman, a bodybuilder?"

"With her Food Lion top and me busy putting in my 'regular customer number' on the keypad, I didn't really examine her."

"But you did see her behind. What did you think? Did you consider 'toe-ing' her a bit?"

He laughed. "No. In fact, I froze, then looked away quickly, always the gentleman."

"The gentleman that time, yes. But you do remember calling me Wonder Woman once, don't you? And not with a gentlemanly intent."

He was clearly surprised. "No, I don't. That might be kind of embarrassing."

"That you forgot? Or that you did it?"

"Probably both."

"It was at that pool party we went to before we were married, the apartment complex where one of my co-workers lived. I had a two-piece, blue and red, and I wore boots with it."

"The image might be coming back."

"Whether it does or not, you thought of me as a fictional creature, not a woman in the flesh. I had become a drawing, a comic book woman."

"You'll have to forgive a much younger man. Right now I'm thinking about how we still view our bodies most of the time with our clothes on. We see ourselves reflected in store windows, friends and relatives show us pictures of ourselves, we take many, many selfies—very few naked."

"Hmm. Well, Narcissus seeing his reflection in a pool is as old as time. Still, you're right that we're not always truthful about what we look like, borrowing images of larger-than-life figures to disguise our flaws, augment our strengths."

"Yes. And for special events, like Independence Day, we dress ourselves up as patriots of one kind or the other—Uncle Sam, Susan B. Anthony, an astronaut."

"We're following in the path of your Mr. Clean and my Wonder Woman."

"Yes. And remember where I started: it's 'in my my pants'--where I and nearly all of our generation keep it most of the time, simply by custom, an inheritance from our Puritan ancestors. We let others imagine it, and we can visualize it ourselves whenever. But, by the way, some us know our skin color is a sign of privilege but others recognize it as a scar. Every once in a while, the curtain drops, and there it is. The bare butt of reality."

Cathy stretched out on the bed. "A foot to the backside, and your eyes go wide. It would be a welcome change if Americans recognized the cultural frames—many of them fictional—which disguise our bodily reality. But now you're going to have me studying all the patriotic garb of our guests and wondering what's underneath!"

"I'll promise to see the Simpson' granddaughter as just another guest of the younger persuasion." He didn't say how he'd view Caro-*lyne* Lee. "And as for your backside . . . " he said with a grin he hoped would be sly.

"That?" Cathy responded with a grin that was indeed sly. "Oh, I left that in a dresser drawer."

Chapter Thirty-eight: Company

When Mark opened the front door on the morning of July 2, a chorus sang out, "The cavalry has arrived!"

He staggered back but managed to swing the door open wider. Bustling about on the porch were his and Cathy's children and grandchildren, eight people in all. Backpacks and coolers and overnight bags were scattered around them on the porch.

And then at his side was Cathy, who had heard the clammer. She immediately knelt to hug her youngest grandchildren—Marcia, 10, and Jennifer 8— who almost knocked her over with their enthusiasm.

"Well, my goodness, it *is* the cavalry!" exclaimed Mark, recovering from shock and sliding into joy. (He suppressed his usual objections to people using the term "cavalry" in a non-military situation and to the fact that they often mispronounced it as "calvary.") "How did you . . ."

Louis laughed. "We were contacted by your friend, Beverly. She said you could use extra hands with this July 4 celebration. But she also thought you would enjoy the surprise, so we didn't call."

"And," added his sister, Mary, "we haven't really had time to pay a good visit lately; so we hope to stay, help clean up, and enjoy your company for a few more days."

"It's a family vacation!" declared Benjamin, the oldest (by a few minutes).

His twin, Susan, added, "We're going to go swimming and crabbing and canoeing . . . but not until after the party, Mom says."

"Okay, okay," Cathy said. "Right now, we need to get you settled in. We have a picnic to go to this afternoon. And then you'll all have big responsibilities tomorrow." With Louis and his wife Brenda, she shepherded the four children upstairs so they could claim beds and put away things.

Mark knew his wife would also be allocating chores for everyone this afternoon and over the next few days. He didn't suspect that she would pull their son over and tell him to buck up his father. She knew this project had gone way beyond what either of them had anticipated. And, she told their son, Mark was also struggling with some demons from his past that had gotten loose in recent days.

Taking Mary and her partner Sandra back to the family room, Mark learned they had been fully briefed about what was to happen. He admitted that he was most nervous about offering a prayer at the AME event. Mary, a regular church-goer, reassured him, "We Episcopalians know there's always something in the *Book of Common Prayer*. I'll text you. And we want you to relax, let us help."

Mary was four years younger than Louis and, because of medical school had started her family later than most of her contemporaries. The maturity she inherited from her mother and her professional achievement produced a calm approach to most things.

"So, when did Beverly contact you about this?" Mark asked.

Mary explained. "It was several weeks ago. She knew we'd need some time to make arrangements. She is a very organized person and, I take it, a good friend now of Mom. She said she should have our contact information just in case. But it was really so she could bring us down."

He chuckled. "Ah! She is thorough. But there are more

folks around here who are less organized—in fact, rather unpredictable. You'll be meeting some of them, and I've learned we'll have to think on our feet.."

"Got it." said Mary. "Now, there's a Charlene, right? Retired, maybe, real estate agent?"

"Real estate development agent. And Marine. She is a mover and a shaker, the one who got us—and, I think, about a dozen other . . . um . . . people not of color—invited to the upriver picnic. And after their event tomorrow, some of them will help transport canopies to Water Street. We're sharing resources."

"And do you know those folks?"

"It's embarrassing to say, no, with a few exceptions. This is a small town, and we see lots of people on Main Street and at the stores out on the bypass. But it seems the races generally socialize separately. Or at least, they have to this point."

"You could be on the forefront of change, then. I'm proud of you."

"It would be more accurate to say I'm being pushed along rather than leading. Charlene and Beverly, who are from this area, are leading a subtle campaign. They've gotten wind of some development schemes being plotted by outsiders. And I think their concerns are important factors in this doubling of events. They want an informed and, they hope, a unified community."

"So, keep our eyes and ears open while we're here, right?"

"To be sure."

The clatter of feet on the stairs signaled that children and possessions were settled upstairs, and a crowd ready to have some fun was descending.

"To the water," called Louis. "We've brought some gear, Dad. In the minivan. Could you bring the tubes and rafts around?"

Mark laughed. "I can if I don't have to blow them up."

Ben volunteered to go with Grandpa and bring the air pump. The others tramped through the kitchen out into the yard. "Follow the path marked by the little flags," Mark auctioned, "if you don't want to sink out of sight or trip over the cypress knees."

He sighed as most ignored them. Still, it was a perfect opportunity for the children, who had already been coated with sunscreen. All of them could swim. And they had four adults keeping an eye on them.

Watching from the deck, Mark read his daughter's text. How she'd found time to send it was a mystery; but he was pleased to read: "Lord God Almighty, in whose Name the founders of this country won liberty for themselves and for us, and lit the torch of freedom for nations then unborn: Grant, we beseech thee, that we and all the people of this land may have grace to maintain these liberties in righteousness and peace; through Jesus Christ our Lord, who liveth and reigneth with thee and the Holy Spirit, one God, for ever and ever. Amen" He would have to carry this spirit into his secret plans for his and Cathy's wedding anniversary on July 5.

At the July 3 picnic the following day the Nelson clan quickly engaged in games of corn hole, badminton, and horseshoes. The younger generation lived in mixed neighborhoods in the suburban area surrounding Norfolk. Their kids went to integrated schools and played sports with friends from different ethnic groups and nationalities. The military presence in Hampton Roads was a multinational one.

Charlene made sure Cathy and Mark spoke with the Reverend Jefferson Douglas and his wife Rebecca, who were ministers at the AME. Mark realized she was "community organizing." As Rebecca and Cathy turned to watch the children playing, Jefferson asked Mark, "You're in the Winston House in town, aren't you?"

He was about Mark's age and had a deliberate, careful manner of speaking. He looked carefully at faces when he spoke. Mark wondered if he was one of those people who can interpret tiny facial muscle movements as expressions of unspoken thought and emotion.

"That's right. We're new to the area, although we've owned the house for five years. Now we're feeling as if we've lived here for more than the first year of our retirement."

"You were smart to come down a number of times before making the move as a permanent change."

"I agree. But I'm beginning to see that I've met only a small portion of the Staffordshire population. You've lived here your whole life?"

"Born in Windsor but left when I was five. My daddy died, and my mother brought us to this county. I've been here the rest of my life, except for four years in the military."

"I had a very short career—two years. I was drafted into the US of Army."

"I was Air Force." He paused to look around. "There's a story there. I was drafted, too, but my uncle, he told me what to do. It was a bad time then, especially for black people."

"Ah." Mark assumed he meant Vietnam, where the percentage of blacks in combat roles—and resulting casualties—was far higher than their percentage in the general population.

"I failed the physical. The next day I drove up to Virginia Beach and volunteered for the Air Force. Became an aircraft mechanic, after a whole lot of training. School around here was not strong for . . . for some of us."

"Did you serve overseas?"

"No. You see, at the end of my first year, they asked me about my father; I said he died when I was five. They asked about my brother; I said I'd never had one."

"Ah, so you were the one male capable of providing for a family. In those days they didn't think a woman could do that, so they weren't going to send you into danger."

"I also think God had other plans for me. And here I am living them."

Looking around at the picnickers, and the game players, and the folks laughing in conversation, Mark thought the Reverend Jefferson Douglas was probably right. He'd served his country honorably. And now he served his people.

Chapter Thirty-nine: Hoo-ah

Mark's Juneteenth prayer was well-received. In fact, everyone in the family was well-received and had a fine time. If, however, Mark had known he would be awakened by He Who Travels Well's crop-smoking, he would have amended the words Mary had sent him—"lit the torch of freedom"—to something like "spread the word of." It seemed in the end, though, that it hadn't been necessary.

Surrounded by family and new friends at the Winston House the next day, he'd settled into his role of Bring Fourth host. With food and drink in place, most guests chatting in the yard, and an American flag flapping lazily on the pole recovered from the garage, Mark cleared his throat and moved to the edge of the deck for his welcoming speech.

Then he saw He Who Travels Well being surrounded by children and some parents in the lower yard. "Uh-oh," he asked himself. "Trouble again?" He sniffed the air for smoke.

There wasn't any. His beekeeper friend called out in a strong voice, "Those younger Americans who'd like to learn some pre-American history, come on down." His voice was carried by the east wind, so Mark and the others could hear him clearly.

"My ancestors," He Who Travels Well explained to his gathering audience of young people and their parents, "kept this a rich and beautiful land to be 'discovered . . . '" (He used finger quotes for the adults.) ". . . by letting it shape their lives rather than trying to bend it to their will." He waved his arms at the river behind him and the ground around him. He was just beyond one of the four large cypress trees which used to mark the river's edge and now stood at the edge of the Nelsons' sometimes soggy lower yard. Little American flags inserted in the ground marked a winding path behind him to the dock.

He went on. "We tended plants that were natural to lowlands and thrived even when storms came in from the ocean. And we accepted the animals who also enjoyed the trees, the fields, the marshes." He looked up toward the sky as if he were about to welcome a prehistoric bird flying down to bring him the gift of a flower. Mark noticed a brown cloth sack lying at his feet.

"One of those creatures was a big—why, it was the largest ever, ever!—a giant honey bee! She was bigger than a robin, bigger than an owl, bigger than . . . ," he gestured. "Bigger than an eagle!" His throat swelled and a buzz came from him and grew louder.

"Oohs" and "aahs" from the children listening, who, too, looked up as if the Mother of all Bees were on her way to them.

"Now this wonderful bee brought many gifts to my people. She taught them how to speak the language of the animals, how to find paths across the swamps, and where the smaller bees kept honey to sweeten their lives. But she asked them one thing in return."

"What was that?" asked the chorus of children who'd moved closer to He Who Travels Well, making a circle around the storyteller.

"She made them promise always to be kind to strangers, to welcome them to their homes, to make them part of their community."

"Oh!"

"That's why, when your ancestors traveled over the seas from distant lands, they were met with gifts from the land and they found new homes here."

"Oh!"

"And that's why today, at a party when we celebrate our country's founding—and its pre-founding—I'm giving each of you a little gift to remember this lesson."

"Oh!"

He pulled from the cloth sack by his feet little bottles of honey, each decorated with a picture of a smiling (very large!) bee and passed them out to eager hands. Then He Who Travels Well looked up to Mark and pointed. "Now, listen to Mr. Nelson, children. He has gifts for you, too, gifts made by your own families and the families of your neighbors."

Making the gesture of hands clapping in appreciation of this unexpected introduction, Mark began, "Good afternoon, friends."

However, the people up on the main lawn had begun to talk among themselves; folks in the side yard milled around the drink coolers; late-comers tried to find places to put their dishes of coleslaw, potato salad, and fruit medleys.

He tried again, a little louder this time. "Good afternoon, friends." A few people close to him looked up, but the majority continued in a party mood.

"Yo!" boomed a powerful voice from the line of cypress forty feet away. "Listen up!" Charlene was in Marine command mode and pointed to Mark. The people did as they were told.

"Welcome, all," resumed Mark, although a bit off his stride. "In just a moment, I will be asking Reverend Baldwin to give us a benediction, and we'll open the food lines. But, as this is Independence Day, I would be remiss if I didn't say a few words about the reasons we are gathering here."

He hesitated, glancing to his right. He had noticed someone making hand gestures at the other end of the deck. Was this person waving at friends, ignoring him? Or directing guests to move or be quiet or take places at the tables? As Mark paused, she—he recognized her as one of guests from yesterday's African Methodist Episcopal Church event—stopped her movements and looked expectantly at him.

He turned back to the crowd. "Now, I'm new to this community. And Cathy and I are honored as newcomers to provide a site for what you've told me is an event that's been celebrated for half a century."

Again, he couldn't help glancing to his right. And this time he understood: this woman was signing his speech! He had no idea that there might be hearing-impaired people here; and even if he had, he wouldn't have thought to seek out someone to sign. But he found this reassuring.

"Of course, I've recognized July 4 since I was a boy growing up in small-town Missouri. I know on this day we honor our nation's founding, the signing of Declaration of Independence. So, I've felt myself part of the United States for—well, longer than half a century."

Again, he felt distracted. The eyes of many seemed focused not on him but on something or someone on his left. He glanced that way to see Raymond Winston standing a step back and a step behind him with a beatific smile on his face and a bottle of beer in his hand.

Mark was determined to go on. "Now, I've not been here in Staffordshire as long as . . . ," he gestured, "as my friend here, Raymond Winston, whose family owned this house, right Ray?"

Ray nodded, smiling at faces he seemed to recognize among those close to the deck. Several of the older guests nodded. He stepped up beside Mark with a slightly unsteady gait, bumping his shoulder lightly.

Ray wore a shirt decorated with red, white, and blue stars and stripes. His pants were faded jungle fatigues, perhaps the same he'd had on when he lay on his back in the old Winston House garage. He also sported an Army boonie hat, standard gear for Vietnam soldiers because they were more comfortable than a helmet in hot and humid climates and provided better protection against rain and sun. Mark hoped a rabbit was not hiding in there.

"Some of you know Ray, I can see," acknowledged Mark. "I first met him when he . . . when he made a rest stop here on his way home from travels."

There were some chuckles, again from the more senior guests. But Ray seemed to take it as a compliment and leaned unsteadily into Mark. He put a hand on his shoulder for support—though it was not clear if the support was for Mark as speaker or for him as unsteady partier.

Mark put his arm around Ray's shoulder. "So, together we're pleased to say—along with He Who Travels Well— this is a community that, in the spirit of our nation's founding, welcomes all to join in the continuing effort to understand and embody democracy."

Ray raised his beer to the crowd and called, "Hoo-ah!" But Mark could see his speech was not inspiring other listeners.

"Our principle of welcoming all to our way of life extends to those who have only known about America from a distance. And because we believe that 'all persons are created equal,' we reach out to those inside our borders as well who haven't enjoyed the opportunities they deserve."

Mark saw from Cathy's expression that he had to bring his remarks to an end with a bit more personal feeling. So, he said, "I had a friend fifty years ago who, sadly, took our freedom farther than he should have. His name was Bruce and he . . . he . . . and he exploded in the air over a country on the other side of the globe. He was a soldier, like Ray and like me."

A more sober look appeared on faces. Ray patted his shoulder.

"What motivated him and . . . and other patriots who put

their lives at risk overseas? It's a belief that we represent the ideals of democracy, the spirit of '76, the desire to be free— even when we can't guarantee them to all."

There were scattered cheers and applause. Ray set his beer bottle down, pulled off his boonie hat, and turned it over. A white bird hopped out and perched on his finger. He lifted his hand and said, "Go free, my little friend." And he did.

At the same moment a whoosh of wings came from the garage loft window as two dozen pigeons rushed out, circled the house, and rose above the cypress. Martina McBride's "Independence Day" played on the sound system. The pigeons/ doves flew higher and wider before heading north and west.

Mark's final words were ready, but he paused because he noted some additional commotion in the lower yard. Heads turned to look. From his vantage point Mark could see Charlene striding to the edge of the water—ignoring, he noted sadly—his flag-marked path to the dock.

Then he saw that "John Smith" was coming ashore again. "Hoo-ah!" the underwater surveillance officer boomed as waves washed around his waist and went on to splash against the bulkhead.

"Hoo-ah!" echoed Charlene and jumped into the water to help him ascend the ladder at the end of the dock.

Forty: Booms

In the kitchen helping Cathy arrange the desserts—pies here, cakes there, whipped and ice cream in a cooler—Mark asked if she didn't think things were going well.

"Not just me," she answered. "The senior seniors from Anne-Harriet's screen porch have all told me we've done a great job. Of course, I had to admit that Beverly was instrumental in getting tables, chairs, canopies (with the help of some AME folks); that our children and their spouses put up the welcoming stand out front to hand out name tags and directions; and that our grandchildren worked hard to make the house and the yard presentable."

"A group effort, to be sure. Now," said Mark, "let me ask you this: have you been seeing people you don't know in the yard with cameras about five times larger than cell phones?"

She smiled. "I believe the Bird Book Club has crashed the party."

Mark shrugged. "Well, our leucistic cardinal is not likely to show up with this chatty crowd milling around the front, side, and back yards."

She smiled. "I saw another person I didn't expect: Les Monroe. He appeared to be a guest of Caro-*lyne*. Want to know what Beverly learned about him?"

"Sure."

"He's an undocumented immigrant from Indonesia. A professional tennis player who overstayed his visa and is trying to remain below ICE's radar."

"Really? We tend to think of Hispanics as the undocumented, but immigrants come here from all parts of the world. I hope it's not a legal obligation for us to report his status."

"Beverley's the lawyer, so I'll defer to her on that question. And I'm deciding to believe he's on some 'road to citizenship.'"

"Speaking of people who might be subject to reporting, though," observed Mark. "I saw Dusty Sherman, who deserved at least a warning for driving an unauthorized vehicle on the streets of Staffordshire."

"Huh," Cathy said, looking around. "I haven't seen him."

Mark chuckled. "It's more likely the Simpsons' granddaughter caught his eye. She wearing very short shorts with tattoos on the backs of her thighs that spell out a message just below the crease at the bottom (so to speak) of each buttock."

"Well, I did see that. It didn't say 'Semper Fie' like Charlene's tattoo, but it did send a message. 'Checky Cheeky.'"

"And she is," agreed Mark. "Well, Dusty must have read it. I saw the two of them slipping up the stairs to make use of . . . opportunity. You can tell Anne-Harriet we failed to follow her instructions regarding free love for young people, but I prefer to stay mum on that one."

"Me, too." She stepped back and surveyed the display of desserts. "It's probably time we mingled a bit. Maybe we can enjoy an 'opportunity' when all this is over." She slapped his behind as she went out the door onto the deck.

Mark went down to the back yard to join a six-person table with the two Reverends Douglas, Charlene, Beverly, and He Who Travels Well. Here, he thought, were the behind-the-scenes power players of Staffordshire. Why not join them?

They were all praising the food, the organization of the event, and the enthusiasm of so many guests. Then discussion turned to the old theater located next to the hardware store on Main Street just a block way. It had been boarded up in the '60s as people preferred to drive to the six-screen movie center in Harbor City. Charlene was asking if they had heard of plans to bring it back.

Beverly looked around to see if anyone else knew anything and then offered, "There is, I think, a group interested in the space as a possible dinner theater and a place for amateur drama."

"If we get Short Bridge replaced," said Rebecca Douglas, "more folks north of the river might come into town for entertainment."

He Who Travels Well pulled his long pipe out of a shoulder bag and began loading it with tobacco. As he struck a match, the whoosh of a rocket taking off from the float boat anchored a hundred yards off the shore interrupted their talk.

They looked in the direction of the sound to see Fireworks Tom standing on the deck of his boat with an old-fashioned megaphone and calling out, "Ahoy, party crowd!" The east wind carried his voice clearly. "Before I put on the first 'green' fireworks show in our lifetimes, you're going to hear from the other of your hosts." He pointed toward the garage.

Cathy was standing in the garage's loft window and waving, first at Tom and then at the guests. "I need to bother y'all for just one moment with a few announcements."

Mark had forgotten how strong her voice was and how confident she was in addressing large groups. According to plan, he began circulating around the crowd and handing out his one-sheet summary of fireworks that are less damaging to plants and animals (including humans), less loud and less bright than traditional explosives, but still capable of creating beauty and spectacle appropriate to the celebration of freedom.

"First," said Cathy from her window perch, one hand holding the rope Beverly had run through a pulley at the end of the extended roof beam." First, if you need to use a restroom, come through the kitchen," she gestured to the door at the back of the deck, "and go down the hall, look right. Second, please put paper and plastic in the appropriate recycling containers; the trash in the cans—both are clearly labeled."

Most people nodded and looked around to identify what she was talking about.

"I have one more item to mention, a little more far-reaching on this anniversary of our country's founding. It won't take me more than two minutes to tell you."

Mark was glad there was no applause at her promise to be brief. In fact, he saw parents directing children to look and to listen.

Cathy continued. "I grew up in southeastern Virginia, in a small town in Norfolk County. It was out of the way for highway travelers, but not for maritime voyagers. It was on the Intercoastal Waterway, a portion of which makes its way down the Currituck and Albemarle Sounds close to us here." She gestured over Tom's boat and down the river.

People nodded their familiarity with how the water connects local towns and counties.

"As children, my friends and I could walk from our neighborhood over to the locks on a canal and watch boats get floated up to go west, floated down to go east. We would see the usual local small boats, but also larger sea-going vessels headed south for Florida and beyond, north to Portsmouth and cities up the East Coast. It was inspirational, connecting us to the faraway and the different."

Mark thought of his own small town on famous Route 66, America's highway to adventure. He suspected everyone, those in big cities and those in small towns, dreamed of what it would be like to travel on a major thoroughfare.

Cathy went on. "We would see barges carrying coal, barrels of oil, machinery; yachts powered by inboard engines, wealthy owners and guests sitting on deck chairs; sailboats with several masts and small life-boats suspended from the stern."

There were nods among the crowd. Most had their own fishing or pleasure crafts. Some had been passengers on the replica of the periauger, the 17th-century boat made from a hollowed-out cypress trunk.

"All my young life," Cathy mused, "I dreamed of journeying on that water to some remote land more glamorous and exciting than the little village where I was. I have traveled and seen some of the world. But what never occurred to me then was to move in a different direction: not up or down the canal, but out from the canal into the neighborhoods close to me that I didn't know. And to do what? To make a difference in the community that nurtured me."

Again, nods. Even the older children seemed to have caught on to the idea of adventure and continued to listen. While Cathy's generation had read books and watched movies, their children and grandchildren played video games, battling dragons in otherworldly landscapes—but all imagined pursuing bright prospects.

"I always thought about what I could gain by traveling away from home. I never thought about what I could do by staying home. Well, now I'm staying in Staffordshire on the

Persimmon River. And I'm asking, not what it can do for me, but what I can do for it."

There was a murmuring of approval. Led by the Reverends' Douglas, a scattered number of African Methodist Episcopal Church members began humming "Lift Every Voice and Sing," The black national anthem had been sung at the earlier Juneteenth celebration. Mark noted that his daughter and her family had joined in.

Cathy concluded, "As we continue a more-than-fifty-year-old tradition of celebrating our past—our many pasts--let us also try to make a brighter, richer future for all in this place. May God bless us and to continue to bless America."

Now there was applause.

Why had he ever doubted her ability to make this event happen? And to hold him together as she did so.

Epilogue: Lighthouses

"You're going to say 'bowdy'--or, knowing you, 'bawdy,'" explained Mark. He spilled the difference. "But the name of this lighthouse we're going to see is pronounced by the locals as "body," which, now that I think of it, may also appeal to you."

Cathy chuckled. "I'm not opposed to 'body,' especially as you advertised this as our deluxe wedding anniversary trip. Why, we're nearly one hundred miles from Staffordshire and so bound to engage in exotic erotic rites."

"Don't make fun. It's not how far we go but how good the trip is. The first item in favor of the overnight is to escape Independence Day."

"Now that seems to me a little like 'No Negativity': getting away from independence almost has to mean finding its opposite--captivity."

Mark raised a finger. "Well, if you're going to characterize marriage as captivity, perhaps. But I prefer to think of the bonds of matrimony as liberating."

"Now, I like that. So, tell me about this lighthouse and the B&B you've reserved for us--not newlyweds— 'oldy-weds?'"

They were driving south on Cape Hatteras National Park Road. Mark agreed to the term: "Yes, oldy-weds. But first, to explain the pronunciation for the lighthouse. This area, the Outer Banks in general, has been called the 'Graveyard of the Atlantic' because there have been so many shipwrecks, resulting in bodies being washed ashore."

"Rough waters. European explorers—and pirates—could run into big storms."

"Correct. I'll have more to say about that it in a minute, but I should point out that The Following Winds B&B is a few blocks east of us right now, on the ocean."

"Oh, so we get look at water!"

"Yes, I know we're always doing that at the Winston House, but we don't have a beach and the waves breaking in front of our deck. And the best part is that it's both a newly-wed and an oldy-wed destination—special meals and other, um, amenities."

"You've piqued my interest. I do hope He Who Travels Well won't be smoking his pipe outside our window."

"Or Raymond performing magic. Conjuring will be my task in the bedroom."

"Ah, for that I guess we should work up an appetite—climbing the lighthouse?"

"By all means. In fact, we have a guided tour beginning in . . ." He checked his watch, "in seven minutes." He pulled into the parking area in front of the lighthouse.

The only visitors on this day, they were soon being led by a man wearing a cap that proclaimed him a "World War II Veteran" and a badge identifying him as "Master Chief Petty Officer Weeks." He told the history of the lighthouse as they worked their way up the 214 steps.

"Now," Weeks began, "this bit of land the lighthouse stands on was called back in 1812 'Bodie's Island' because a nearby barrier island was owned by the family of the same name. But," he raised a finger, and turned around to face the Nelsons, "the Roanoke Inlet closed at one point, and the barrier island was connected to Currituck Banks, the peninsula to the north that runs all the way up into Virginia."

"So," questioned Mark, "while we call this the 'Bodie Island Lighthouse,' it sits on the peninsula, not a separate piece of land surrounded by water?"

"Right you are, though, this isn't the original lighthouse you're climbing. You see, back in 1837, one Lieutenant Napoleon L. Coste of Campbell concluded that more ships met their end here than any other spot along the Atlantic. So, he convinced the federal government to build a lighthouse that could guide crews around the cape."

"Good for him," smiled Cathy, charmed by their "senior" senior guide and wanting to charm him also.

"Yes, he made a sound--so to speak--proposal, but the man who supervised the first building, 54 feet high and finished in 1847, used a brick foundation that rested on nothing but sand. It started leaning within two years. In fact, I myself have seen signs of the original faulty construction under water as recently as two years ago."

"With those waves crashing in right now," said Cathy, "I don't see how they'd still be here."

"Lighthouse location is a bit complicated, as you'll learn. But the collapse of the first lighthouse is the kind of thing that happens when you take control from the military and give it to civilians. I saw that in my nearly forty years with the Navy and the Coast Guard, another twenty-five as a DOD contractor."

"That's a long career!" exclaimed Mark. "Were you stationed at the base in Harbor City. That's a major East Coast facility, I understand."

"One of the busiest in the country. Operations reach as far as Greenland and the Caribbean. My first duty station was nearby, with the Naval Air Station in Weeksville, 1943. We sent blimps out to look out for enemy submarines."

"I guess you've seen a lot, then, in your lifetime," noted Cathy. "It's good that you're still contributing."

"It's what we do, ma'am." It wasn't clear who "we" were, but Mark felt the term could include the Martins and the Petersons in Staffordshire. And someone else whose name wouldn't come up right then.

"Watch yourself here," the veteran advised as they stepped

into the glassed-in room at the top of the stairs."

When he turned around to inspect the light, Mark leaned close to Cathy and whispered, "Does he remind you of someone?"

She opened her eyes wide.

Weeks went on. "A second lighthouse was finished in 1859, but it came down even more quickly than the first and not from natural causes."

"The Civil War?" proposed Mark.

"Right again. Southern forces thought that that construction, 80 feet tall, would be used by the enemy. So, they blew it up in 1861."

"Speaking of blowing things up, the wind is pretty fierce out there," said Mark, looking out from the observatory and seeing rolling whitecaps.

"We could have a storm tonight, to be sure," said Chief Petty Officer Weeks. "But rest assured, this version of Brodie's Island Lighthouse is solid. This third Brodie's Island Lighthouse was built in 1871-72. And in the last decade, the building has been reinforced by the National Park Service."

"Was there a keeper to run the station?" asked Cathy.

"Yes, though it was a hard life: the site was isolated, and you could only get out here by boat. If the keeper had family, they stayed over on Roanoke Island except for the summer. But in 1932 everything was electrified. And now, of course, satellites keep ships aware of conditions at sea. Although this still shines," he tapped the light, "it's more a park feature than a functioning lighthouse.

Where do you live, Master Chief?" asked Cathy as they

wound their way down toward the bottom. "I take it, not on the premises like keepers in the past."

"No," he chuckled. "Me and the missus—like the lighthouses, she's my third—have a little cottage up in Nags Head. I just do the tour one day a week."

"Well," smiled Mark. "You do it very well, and we thank you. If there were a tavern next door, I'd buy you a beer to show my gratitude."

"Suzie is here to take me home to a brew and a meal, but thank you. You'll be raising your glass at the Following Winds, I'm told, and a fine meal will follow."

He touched his hat in a kind of salute and turned toward the parking lot. Mark and Cathy could see a much younger woman waving at him from a jeep.

They watched him move with more speed than they would have expected from a 90-something-year-old who'd just climbed a lighthouse.

"Did he remind you of someone?" asked Mark.

Cathy laughed. "John Smith! I thought of it thirty minutes ago. But right now, let's get to the Following Winds before the winds chase us out to sea."

The clouds to the west did threaten a coming storm. Their B & B, though, an old farm building that had been moved to its current site, was snug and tight.

Later, they sat, stuffed, in their room's two matching stuffed chairs, recovering from over-indulgence in a down-home Southern dinner: fresh crab, grilled bay scallops, fried flounder; coleslaw from the inn's garden; home-made hush puppies, and a splendid apple pie. Mark cleared his throat.

"The fact that Brodie's Island is not really an island reminds me."

She looked at him. "Are you going to give me your 'no man is an island ask not for whom the bell tolls' speech?"

John Donne's 17th-century poem was a favorite of Mark's, and he began to recite the famous lines: "No man is an island, / Entire of itself, / Every man is a piece of the continent, / A part of the main."

"Very nice," Cathy said. "And appropriate to the occasion, as we presently stand—well, sit—on a peninsula connected to a continent."

"Well, I offer it once more as a kind of apology . . . for being . . . in the last weeks a bit difficult. I think I was wanting to be an island and not part of the mainland."

"I accept that, if it means you'll be more even-tempered in the future. Now, you do know, though, how Donne's words apply to Brodie's Island in a second way?"

"Well, uh, of course, I do, but go ahead and remind me." He often said this when he didn't know; but she knew he didn't know; and he knew she . . . .

"Well, you've always called it a 'poem,'" she explained. "But the original words come from one of Donne's sermons. He became an Anglican priest because the Catholic tradition he was raised in was persecuted in that era of religious controversy."

"So, his title wasn't quite right, and his literary work is misnamed, by me at least. But his words are immortal, however we classify them."

"Agreed." She sighed and rose. "So, let us make the long

journey from chair to bed lest we 'clods be washed away by the sea.'"

"I think I can make it. I'm afraid, though the magic of Mark the Magnificent will have to wait for the morning."

His Lovely Assistant only smiled and took his hand.

The End

Enjoy this preview of *School: the natural order*. Novel Three in the Persimmon River Series. Coming in 2025.

Chapter One: Left-hearted

"I have news," said Cathy Nelson to her husband when she came home after what was supposed to be a routine check-up with her primary caregiver. The newly retired couple lived in Staffordshire, a village of 2000 nestled on a bay of a North Carolina Tidewater river.

Mark tensed. Bad news about health could come any moment at their age.

Cathy explained, "I've just learned that my IVC (inferior vena cava) is on the left side, not the right as it is for more than 99.5% of all people."

"What does that mean?" Mark asked. "I don't even know what an IVC is."

"It's this major blood vessel in the middle of the body—mine is on the wrong side. All the blood in my—well, and yours, too--our trunk, abdomen, the pelvis and legs—is carried to the right atrium of the heart by this, I guess, giant tube."

Mark resisted seeing this as upsetting. He felt they'd made the transition from long, busy careers to the slower pace of village life. Now he wanted to maintain that sense of ease. "And how," he asked, "is it that you're just discovering this anatomical reality now when it must have been this way from birth, rather than transposing itself one day when it was bored?"

"Oh, it functions just fine, but you don't see what this means: it means I'm left-hearted!"

He did not know what that meant but connected it vaguely to left-handedness (which, he'd heard, artistic people tend to be) or left-leaning (as if politics were genetic). "Do I need to adjust all the furniture in the house, including our marriage bed, to accommodate this oddity?"

"I don't think so, but I'm still learning about it. You recall the aortic aneurysm scan I had last week," she explained. "It showed this long-hidden truth about me."

"You do have the thing, the IVC, though, don't you?"

She frowned. "The aorta is on the right side. For all normal people, the IVC is more or less in front of it. But my IVC is on the left side of my body, way the heck from where it's supposed to be, back-ass-wards."

"Well, you've been that way forever, I guess, and you seem to function just fine."

"Don't be so sure. The way I see it, some of my circuits are crossed; I have been internally mis-wired since birth, before then, I guess. Who knows what this has done or will do to me?"

It irritated Cathy when Mark, typical man, dismissed her health concerns, especially as she'd been a registered nurse, a hospital floor captain, a program administrator. Men never overcame the sense of inadequacy in not being able to give birth.

She had wondered, in fact, on the drive home from the clinic if this misplaced inferior vena cava had doomed her to an inferior fate that was about to bring tragedy.

She snapped at Mark, "If my stupid IVC had been on the right side, where it was supposed to be, my entire life could have taken a different course."

She was not going to press the point right then, but she was more shaken than her jokes revealed—but not by her wrongly positioned IVC. She had had a call out of nowhere from an old nursing school friend that reminded her of alternative destinies. The recent mishap of a purple martin chick added to Cathy's vague anxiety.

Cathy had a special affinity for the purple martin, who migrated from the Amazon every spring to Tidewater communities in North Carolina and other East Coast states, returning in late summer. They rode the air currents as if they had built-in GPS's that charted a precise path across the heavens, no training or guidance needed.

Cathy celebrated their arrival in April, perhaps because the species shared a name with her nursing school friend, Martin Waters. The bird's sweptback, pointed wings, the dark purple sheen of plumage, and alert, quick eyes matched the young woman's slim, small frame, sleek black hair, the bright interested look.

Cathy was drawn to (all) the [M]martins' journeys: the birds from the northern Amazon basin to the northeastern American states and back; the girl's from Norfolk County, Virginia, to Central America and . . . well back, but not quite the same as the person who went. Cathy still sorrowed about losing Martin to . . . what? The forces of history, perhaps.

Martin reminded Cathy of Raymond Winston, another military veteran who's been knocked off course by travel. A Staffordshire native who fought in Vietnam, he came and went from his hometown, but on a less regular schedule than migrating birds. He'd been more stable in recent years after his one-time girlfriend Dolly reappeared in his life.

"I'd like you to meet Trixie," he had said just this week, waving a hand by his side to indicate a scruffy, Benji-type dog on the Nelson's front porch. "She's really Dolly's dog, but she's staying with me while Dolly visits an old friend in Knoxville."

"Well, come in, then," said Cathy, stepping back to give them room.

"Trixis is . . . um, house trained, I assume?" asked Mark.

"Not just house trained my friend, but trained as a magician's assistant." Raymond claimed to perform as an amateur conjurer.

Trixie trotted ahead of Raymond down the hall to the kitchen/family of the two-story frame house on Water Street, seeming to know where she was and what her role would be.

"Oh, dear," said Mark to himself.

"How interesting," said Cathy, following Trixie and leading the two men. "Will you show us some of her tricks."

"Of course," smiled Raymond. "Not that she is going to take your place as my North Carolina Lovely Assistant. I see her as part of our growing troupe."

Mark was the last to enter the family room/kitchen and looked around for Trixie. "Where did she go, Ray?" he asked. "Is she your 'disappearing lady'?"

He was referring to an act in which the lady's clothes disappeared, but she did not. Mark claimed it was a striptease, but the Conjuror insisted it was an industry standard and one of his favorite illusions.

Ray was scanning the room himself, which was divided by a long counter into a slim kitchen area and a large family room with sofa, loveseat, two rocking chairs, and a table for six in front of the bay windows that looked out on the Persimmon River. "Huh," he said. "She does do this—here one minute, somewhere else the next. Trixie," he called. "Come."

There was the sound of toenails clipping in the hall, and the dog trotted into the room—smiling, it seemed to Cathy.

Mark decided not to ask how Trixie had slipped past them back into the main part of the house, suspecting that Ray's explanation would be as evasive as his explanation of other tricks.

"Would she like water?" offered Cathy. "I'm afraid we don't have any dog treats."

"She'll ask when she needs something," Ray said. "And right now I want to tell you a bit of her history, as it's a fascinating story. In the meantime, though, a cup of coffee would be nice for me."

It would prove an unsettling tale and became linked in Cathy's thoughts to local dangers: like the snakes, owls, cats, and turtles that were her pursuing her purple martins. Each predator reminded Cathy of threats her friend Martin had faced in her military career.

Over the past week Cathy and Mark had been watching the parent birds coax fledglings out of the house at the river's edge. The chicks would learn to hunt on their own for mosquitos and other bugs. But they were hunted, too.

One little bird seemed not up to the task of strong flight, dipping down from the fifteen-foot-high house to bounce along the river's surface like a water skier about to cartwheel into the waves. She ended up floundering against the bulkhead at the edge of the Nelson's property. Large snapping turtles swam beneath the surface and could drag down goslings, baby ducks, and other small waterfowl.

Cathy sprinted down to the bulkhead to lift the little martin up on the grass. "She'll rest a bit, get her strength, join her brothers and sisters for the long journey south," she had insisted.

The discovery of her own left-heartedness, however, would make her lose confidence in the structured world of retirement. She thought of martin the wayward bird and Martin the struggling friend as signs that she had moved on to a different, difficult path without being aware of it, rerouted by anatomy.

In retirement she and Mark enjoyed the end of professional training and assessment, license renewals, repetitive verifications, measurement and documentation. But in the weeks ahead they would be reminded that education never ends, even if it's not housed in a building. Cathy would conclude that her left-heartedness had hidden elements in her personal and the community's history that would shape her senior years in unexpected ways.

. . . to be continued.

About the Author

Taylor Curtis is a pen name for Michael Lund, who lives in south central Virginia and, with friends and family, spends many weekends and much of the summer in an old home in northeastern North Carolina. Professor Emeritus of English at Longwood University, he was a US Army correspondent at Fort Campbell, KY (1969-79) and in South Vietnam (1970-71). In addition to having published scholarly books and articles about 19th-and

Photo by Michael Niver

20th-century British and American literature, he is the author of novels inspired by Route 66, America's Mother Road. He has also produced two collections of short stories: *How to Not Tell a War Story* (2012) and *Eating With Veterans* (2015). Lund also directs Home and Abroad, a free writing program for military, veterans, and family, in rural central Virginia.

Several dozen of his recent short stories reflecting military experience have appeared in contemporary journals, including "Left-Hearted," *Line of Advance* (2016); reprinted in *Our Best War Stories: An Anthology of Darron L. Wright Award Winners*. Middle West Press (October 2020)

Scan the QR code to go to the website.

The author may be contacted: lundmc@longwood.edu.